" *Flowers, Plants and Fishes, Birds, Beasts, Flyes,
    and Bees,*
  *Hils, Dales, Plaines, Pastures, Skies, Seas, Rivers,
    Trees,*
  There's nothing neere at hand, or farthest sought,
  But with the needle may be shap'd and wrought."

—JOHN TAYLOR (" The Praise of the Needle ").

EMBROIDERY AND TAPESTRY
WEAVING

Frontispiece   *See page* 249.

EMBROIDERY AND TAPESTRY WEAVING

A PRACTICAL TEXT-BOOK
OF DESIGN AND WORKMANSHIP
BY GRACE CHRISTIE WITH
DRAWINGS BY THE AUTHOR
AND OTHER ILLUSTRATIONS

PITMAN · LONDON
TAPLINGER · NEW YORK
A PENTALIC BOOK

PITMAN PUBLISHING LIMITED
39 Parker Street, London WC2B 5PB

Associated Companies
Copp Clark Pitman, Toronto
Pitman Publishing New Zealand Ltd, Wellington
Pitman Publishing Pty Ltd, Melbourne

Published simultaneously in the USA by Taplinger
Publishing Company Inc, 200 Park Avenue South,
New York, N.Y. 10003

First published in Great Britain, 1906
Fourth Edition 1915, reprinted 1920, 1924, 1928, 1933
First published in paperback 1979

UK ISBN 0 273 01266 5
US ISBN 0-8008-2401-6

Reproduced and printed by photolithography in
Great Britain at The Pitman Press, Bath

EDITOR'S PREFACE

NEEDLEWORK, which is still practised traditionally in every house, was once a splendid art, an art in which English workers were especially famous, so that, early in the XIIIth century, vestments embroidered in England were eagerly accepted in Rome, and the kind of work wrought here was known over Europe as "English Work." Embroideries *façon d'Angleterre* often occupy the first place in foreign inventories.

At Durham are preserved some beautiful fragments of embroidery worked in the Xth century, and many examples, belonging to the great period of the XIIIth and XIVth centuries, are preserved at the South Kensington Museum, which is particularly rich in specimens of this art. In order to judge of what were

then its possibilities it is worth while
to go and see there three notable copes,
the blue cope, the Sion cope, and the
rose-colour Jesse-tree cope, the last two
of which are certainly English, and the
former probably so. The Sion cope
bears a remnant of an inscription which
has unfortunately been cut down and
otherwise injured, so that all that I have
been able to read is as follows: DAVN
PERS: DE: V . . .; probably the name of
the donor.

In the XIIIth century the craft of
embroidery was practised both by men
and women.

That great art patron, Henry the
Third, chiefly employed for his embroideries, says Mr. Hudson Turner, "a
certain Mabel of Bury St. Edmund's,
whose skill as an embroideress seems to
have been remarkable, and many interesting records of her curious performances
might be collected." And I have found
a record of an embroidered chasuble made
for the king by "Mabilia" of St. Edmund's
in 1242. The most splendid piece of
embroidery produced for this king must
have been the altar frontal of Westminster Abbey, completed about 1269.

It was silk, garnished with pearls, jewels, and translucent enamels. Four embroideresses worked on it for three years and three-quarters, and it seems to have cost a sum equal to about £3000 of our money.

"The London Broderers" did not receive a formal charter of incorporation until 1561, but they must have been a properly organised craft centuries before. In 2 Henry IV. it was reported to Parliament that divers persons of the "Craft of Brauderie" made unfit work of inferior materials, evading the search of "the Wardens of Brauderie" in the said City of London.

In Paris, in the year 1295, there were ninety-three embroiderers and embroideresses registered as belonging to the trade. The term of apprenticeship to the craft was for eight years, and no employer might take more than one apprentice at a time. In the XVIth century the Guild was at the height of its power, and embroideries were so much in demand that the Jardin des Plantes in Paris was established to furnish flower-subjects for embroidery design. It was founded by the gardener, Jean Robin, and by Pierre Vallet, "brodeur" to Henry IV. In the XVIIIth century the company numbered 250 past-masters.

To this craft the present volume forms, I believe, an admirable introduction and text-book, not only on the side of workmanship, but also on that difficult subject, "design"—difficult, that is, from its having been so much discussed in books, yet entirely simple when approached, as here, as a necessary part of workmanship. It is fortunate that we have not as yet learned to bother our cooks as to which part of their work is designing and which is merely mechanical. Of course the highest things of design, as well as of workmanship, come only after long practice and to the specially gifted, but none the less every human creature must in some sort be a designer, and it has caused immense harm to raise a cloud of what Morris called "sham technical twaddle" between the worker and what should be the spontaneous inspiration of his work. What such combination has produced in past times, may perhaps best be understood by some reading in old church inventories of the simply infinite store of magnificent embroidered vestments which once adorned our churches. In an in-

ventory of Westminster Abbey I find
mentioned such patterns as roses and
birds, fleur-de-luces and lybardes, angels
on branches of gold, roses and ships, eagles
and angels of gold, castles and lions, white
harts, swans, dogs, and antelopes.

W. R. LETHABY.

AUTHOR'S PREFACE

In the following pages the practical sides of Embroidery and Tapestry Weaving are discussed, their historical development being only incidentally touched upon.

The drawings illustrating design and the practical application of stitches have been taken almost without exception from actual Embroidery or Tapestry; the exceptions, where it has been impossible to consult originals, from photographic representations obtained from various sources, among which the collection of M. Louis de Farcy should be mentioned.

I have to thank Miss May Morris and Mrs. W. R. Lethaby for permission to reproduce pieces of their work, and Miss Killick, Colonel J. E. Butler-Bowdon,

xvii

Author's
Preface

the Viscount Falkland, and the Reverend F. J. Brown of Steeple Aston for permission to reproduce work in their possession. Also I must thank the authorities of the Victoria and Albert Museum for help in various ways, and Mr. J. H. Taylor, M.A. Oxf. and Cam., for his kindness in reading the proofs.

GRACE CHRISTIE.

Ewell.

CONTENTS

PART I

EMBROIDERY

CHAPTER I

CHAPTER II

TOOLS, APPLIANCES, AND MATERIALS

CHAPTER III

PATTERN DESIGNING

CHAPTER IV

STITCHES

CHAPTER V

STITCHES—(*continued*)

CHAPTER VI

STITCHES—(*continued*)

CHAPTER VII

CANVAS WORK AND STITCHES

CHAPTER VIII

METHODS OF WORK

CHAPTER IX

METHODS OF WORK—(*continued*)

CHAPTER X

METHODS OF WORK—(*continued*)

CHAPTER XI

EMBROIDERY WITH GOLD AND SILVER THREADS

CHAPTER XII

LETTERING, HERALDRY, AND EMBLEMS

CHAPTER XIII

THE GARNITURE OF WORK

CHAPTER XIV

PRACTICAL DIRECTIONS

PART II

TAPESTRY WEAVING

CHAPTER XV

CHAPTER XVI

NECESSARY APPLIANCES AND MATERIALS

CHAPTER XVII

PREPARATIONS FOR WORK

CHAPTER XVIII

THE TECHNIQUE OF WEAVING

PART I
EMBROIDERY

PART I—EMBROIDERY

CHAPTER I

INTRODUCTION

In the practice of embroidery the needle- woman has an advantage not now shared by workers in any other craft, in that the technical processes are almost a matter of inherited skill. Every woman can sew, and it is with little more than the needle and thread, which she habitually employs, that the greatest masterpieces of the art have been stitched. The art of embroidery, however, is not merely an affair of stitches; they are but the means by which ideas can be expressed in intelligible form, and memories of all kinds of things be pictured on stuffs.

To laboriously train the hand is scarcely worth while unless it is capable of expressing something that is at least pretty. Nowadays much embroidery is done with the evident intent of putting into it the minimum expenditure of both thought and labour, and such work furnishes but a poor ideal to fire the enthusiasm of the novice; happily, there still exist many fine examples showing what splendid results may be achieved; without some knowledge of this work we cannot obtain a just idea of the possibilities of the art.

It is obvious that much advantage can be gained from studying the accumulated experience of the past in addition to that current in our own day. To do this intelligently, the history of embroidery must be followed in order that the periods richest in the various kinds of work may be ascertained. Museums afford useful hunting-grounds for the study of past work; other sources are private collections, churches, costume in pictures or on engraved brasses, and manuscript inventories such as those of cathedral treasuries, which sometimes contain interesting detailed descriptions of their embroidered vestments and hangings.

Blind copying of old work is not of much value; it is not possible or desirable

28

to imitate XIIIth century work now,
but much can be learned by examining
fine examples in an appreciative and ana-
lytical spirit. In what way the design has
been built up can be discovered; the most
complicated result may often be resolved
into quite elementary lines. The student
must find out wherein lie the attraction
and interest, note good schemes of colour,
and learn about stitches and methods of
work by close examination of the embroidery, both front and back.

Every one knows what embroidery is,
and a formal definition seems unnecessary.
As a matter of fact, it would be a difficult
task to give one, since weaving, lace-
making, and embroidery are but subtle
variations of the same art.

This art may be of the highest or the
most homely character, and the latter is by
no means to be despised. Simple unaffected
work decorating the things of every-day
use can give a great deal of pleasure in
its way. This should surely be the accomplishment of every woman, for though
she may not have the skill to attain to the
highest branches, it would at least enable
her to decorate her home with such things
as the counterpanes, curtains, and other

objects that set such a personal stamp upon the English domestic work of several centuries, and which nowadays can hardly be found except stored up in museums.

It is advisable as a general rule that the design be both made and carried out by the same person. From the worker's own point of view the interest must be much greater when working out her own ideas than when merely acting as amanuensis to another. The idea is more likely to be expressed with spirit; further there is the possibility of adding to or altering, and thereby improving, the work as it progresses. The designer must in any case be well acquainted with stitches and materials, for they play an important part in achieving good results. The individuality of the worker should be evident in her work; indeed it generally is, for even plain hems by two people bear quite different characters; the degree of individuality present, varies with each one, but in any case it will be much more marked if the design and stitching bear the stamp of the same personality.

The difference between good and unsatisfactory results should be carefully

thought out, for it is often but a small
matter. The best kind of work is that
which appeals to the intelligence as well
as to the eye, which is another way of
saying there should be evidence of mind
upon the material. Work must be interesting in some way if it is to be attractive;
it had better almost be faulty and interesting than dull, dry, and correct. It can
interest by reminding us of pleasant things,
such as familiar flowers, shady woods, or
green lawns; birds, beasts, and so forth
can be depicted in their characteristic atti-
tudes, or a story can be told; in fact,
work can be made attractive in a hundred
different ways. It must not show signs
of having wearied the worker in the doing;
variety and evidence of thought lavishly
expended upon it will prevent this, and
enthusiasm will quicken it with life.

The selection of the object to work
comes at an early stage, and is a matter
to be well considered, for it is a pity to
spend time and labour upon unsuitable
objects when there are many excellent ones
to choose from. In thinking over what
to work it should be realised that it takes
no longer to execute one rather important
piece than several of a less ambitious

31

character, and that the former is generally more worth the doing. Whether the subject is a suitable one for embroidery or not sometimes depends upon the method chosen for carrying it out; for instance, anything that has to endure hard wear must be treated in such a way as to stand it well.

Dress is a fine subject for embroidery; but, for the decoration to be satisfactory, the art of designing dress must be understood, and the dress must also be well cut, or the embroidery will be quite wasted upon it. What is termed "art dress," proverbially bad, well deserves its reputation. There is a great difference in the quantity of work that may be put into dress decoration; this may be simply an embroidered vest, collar, and cuffs, or it may be actually an integral part of the costume, which as a much bigger and more difficult undertaking is correspondingly finer in effect when successfully carried out.

Amongst larger objects that well repay the labour of embroidery, hangings of various kinds, quilts, screens, furniture coverings, altar frontals, church vestments, may be mentioned; amongst smaller, are bags, boxes, book-covers, gloves or mittens,

bell-pulls, cushions, mirror frames, all
kinds of household linen, infants' robes,
and so on, and for church use such things
as alms-bags, book-markers, stoles, pulpit
and lectern frontals. Then a panel may
be worked with the deliberate intention
of framing it to hang on a wall. There
is no reason why the painter should have
the monopoly of all the available wall
space, for decorative work is undoubtedly
in place there; a piece of embroidered
work might well fill a panel over a
mantel-piece. There is no need to discuss
what not to do, but, if the attraction to
embroider a tea-cosy is too strong to
resist, it should surely be of washable
materials.

Embroidery has distinct practical advantages over some other crafts practised
nowadays—no special studio need be
devoted to its use, for most work can be
done in any well-lighted room, which
indeed will be rendered more attractive
by the presence of an embroidery frame,
for this is in itself a characteristic and
dainty piece of furniture. It need but
seldom interfere with one of our pleasant
traditions, genial converse with, and about,
our neighbours, for it is a distinctly

33

sociable occupation. Work of this kind can be put down and taken up at leisure; the necessary outlay in materials need not be extravagant, and so on. Many other points might be thought of, but the claims of the art do not demand any special pleading, for it is pleasant in the actual working, and can produce an infinite variety of most interesting results.

CHAPTER II

TOOLS, APPLIANCES, AND MATERIALS

Needles—Scissors—Thimbles—Frames—Stand and Frame combined — Tambour Frame — Cord-making Appliance—Requisites for Transferring Patterns — Pricker — Knife — Spindle — Piercer —Suitable Materials for Embroidering upon— Threads of all Kinds—Stones, Beads, &c.

Tools, Appliances, and Materials

GOOD workmanship takes a prominent, though not the first, place. Technical excellence in needlework, as in all other artistic crafts, is a question of the worker's perseverance and her ability in the use of tools. In embroidery these are few and simple, and are as follows :—

34

Needles.—For most purposes needles known as long-eyed sharps are used. Tapestry needles, similar to these, but with blunt points, are useful for canvas work and darned netting. For gold work a special needle can be procured with sharp point and long wide eye. A bent needle makes a crooked stitch; but needles if made of good steel should not bend; they break if used unfairly. The eye should be cleanly cut, or it roughens the thread. The needle must be just stout enough to prepare for the thread an easy passage through the material.

Scissors.—Three pairs may be necessary; for ordinary work a small pair with fine sharp points, for gold work small ones with strong points similar to nail scissors, and for cutting-out purposes a large pair with one rounded and one sharp point.

Thimbles.—Steel ones are said to be most serviceable, silver are most usual; but whatever the material they must be neatly made in order not to wear the thread.

Frames.—A common type of frame is shown at fig. 1. It is made in various sizes; the one here represented measures

35

18 inches across. It consists of four pieces of wood, two rollers for the top and base and two side pieces. Each of the rollers has a piece of webbing securely nailed along it, and its extremities are

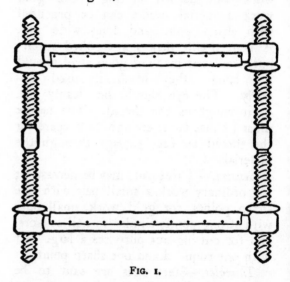

FIG. 1.

pierced with holes to receive the side pieces. These are formed of two long wooden screws, fitted with movable nuts, which adjust the width of the frame and the tautness of the stretched work. The piece of material that is stretched between

36

is the link that keeps the frame together, for the screw ends fit just loosely in the holes of the rollers. The side pieces are sometimes made of flat laths of wood pierced with holes at regular intervals; in these are inserted metal pins, by means of which the work is kept stretched. Fig. 9 represents a frame of this type. If the frame is a very large one it can have a strengthening bar fixed across the centre from roller to roller.

The frame is most convenient for work when fixed in a stand, although it can be used leaning against a table or the back of a chair. A very large frame would be supported upon trestles, but for ordinary purposes, a stand, such as the one shown in fig. 2, is practical. It consists of two upright wooden posts, a little over 2 feet in height, which are connected near the base by a strengthening cross piece. Both this and the uprights are adjustable; the centre part of the posts is arranged to slide up and down, and can be fixed at any convenient height by the insertion of a long metal pin; the width of the cross piece is regulated in similar fashion, being made firm, by a screw, at the required width, thus allowing various sized frames to be

used in the same stand. The frame is

FIG. 2.

fixed in place by metal clamps, and a
wooden pivot is arranged so as to permit

the stretched work to be inclined at any angle convenient. Both stand and frame should be well made and of good wood, for they must be able to stand strain and be perfectly firm and true when fixed for work.

A small circular frame, such as is shown in fig. 3, is useful for marking linen or for any small work. This, formed of two hoops fitting closely one within the other, can be procured in wood, ivory, or bone, of various sizes, the one illustrated being about 6 inches in diameter. The material to be worked upon

FIG. 3.

is stretched between these hoops like the parchment on a drum. These tambour frames, as they are called, are sometimes fixed into a small stand or fitted with a wooden clamp for fastening to a table; this frees both hands for work. These tambours cannot well be recommended; the material is apt to stretch unevenly, and a worked part, if flattened between the hoops, is liable to be damaged.

The illustration at fig. 4 shows a simple

little instrument for making a twisted cord. It is interesting to note that Etienne Binet, who wrote on embroidery about 1620, when discussing some necessary equipment for an embroideress mentions "*un rouet pour faire les cordons.*"

There is sometimes a difficulty in procuring the cord just right to suit the finished work; the texture may be too coarse to put beside fine embroidery, it may not be a good match, and, even if so at first, it may fade quite differently from the worked silks. For these and other reasons it is a safe method to make the cord one's self, possibly with some materials of the kind already used in the embroidery.

This appliance enables the worker to make any kind of twisted cord; it is as simple as a toy to handle, and gives excellent results. It is a metal instrument about 8 inches in height. The three small discs are wheels, supported on the arms of an upright cross which has a heavy circular base. These three wheels are connected by a cord with a larger wheel below that has a handle attached to it. The cord runs in a groove round the circumference of each wheel,

40

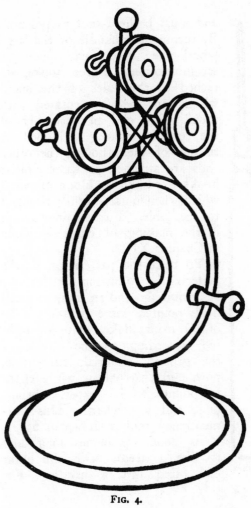

FIG. 4.

41

and must be held taut in position. By turning the handle of the large wheel the three small ones are set in motion. Three hooks, attached to the axles of the small wheels, are therefore rotated with them. One end of each ply of the cord in making is looped on to one of these hooks, the other ends are attached to three similar hooks fixed into a block of wood which, when in use, is firmly clamped to the table. Further instruction in the making of cords is given in Chapter XIII.

To trace the pattern on to the material the following articles may be required: Indian ink, a small finely-pointed sable brush, a tube of oil paint, flake white or light red, according to the colour of the ground material, turpentine, powdered charcoal or white chalk for pounce, tracing paper, drawing-pins, and a pricker. This last-mentioned tool is shown in fig. 5. It is about 5 inches long, and is like a needle with the blunt end fitted into a handle. For

FIG. 5.

42

rubbing on the pounce some soft clinging
material rolled into a ball is necessary.
A piece of old silk hose tightly rolled up
makes an excellent pad for the purpose.

The knife shown in fig. 6 is useful
for cutting out at times when the use
of scissors is not practical. It is used
in an upright position, with the point
outwards.

A spindle for winding gold thread

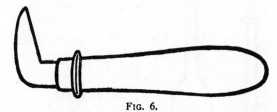

FIG. 6.

upon whilst working is shown in fig. 7.
It is about 8 inches long. A soft padding
of cotton thread is first placed round
(between A and B, fig. 7), and the gold
thread wound upon that. The end of the
thread passes through the forked piece at
the top on its way to being worked into the
material. The use of this or some similar
appliance enables the worker to avoid much
touching of the metal threads.

A small tool called a piercer is repre-

43

sented by fig. 8 ; it is used in gold work ; the flat end assists in placing the gold in position, and also in making the floss silk lie quite flat ; the pointed end is used for piercing holes in the material for passing coarse thread to the back, and for other purposes. This little tool, made of steel, is about 5 inches in length.

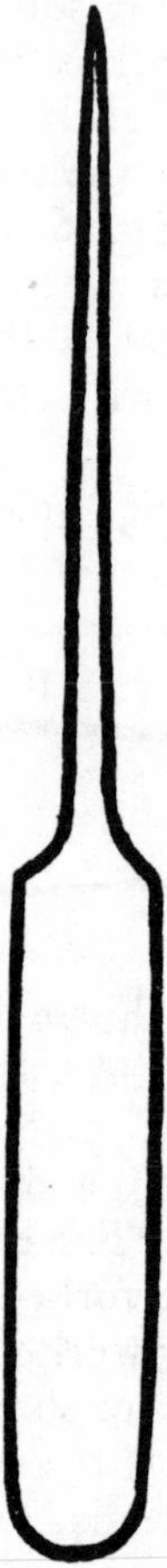

MATERIALS

The surface is a matter of special interest in embroidery work. This makes the choice of materials of great importance. Besides the question of appearance, these must be suitable to the purpose, durable, and, if possible, pleasant to work with and upon. The materials chosen

FIG. 7.   FIG. 8.

44

should be the best of their kind, for time and labour are too valuable to be spent upon poor stuffs; occasionally a piece of old work is seen with the ground material in shreds and the embroidery upon it in a good state of preservation, which

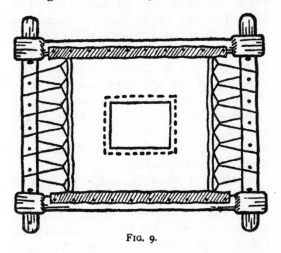

FIG. 9.

is a pity, for a newly applied ground of any kind is never as satisfactory as the original one. Still another plea for the use of good materials is the moral effect they may have upon the worker, inciting her to put forth her best efforts in using them.

45

The purpose to which the work is to be put usually decides the ground material, besides governing pattern, stitches, and everything else. A background is chosen, as a rule, to show to advantage and preserve what is to be placed upon it, though sometimes it is the other way about, and the pattern is planned to suit an already existing ground.

A background must take its right place, and not be too much in evidence, although if of the right kind it may be full of interest. There are, roughly speaking, three ways of treating the ground, leaving the material just as it is, covering part of it with stitching, or working entirely over it.

If there is no work upon the ground the choice of material becomes more important. Texture, colour, tone, and possibly pattern, have all to be considered, though the problem is often best solved by the selection of a plain white linen. The question of texture is sometimes one of its suitability for stitching upon; colour and tone may be of all kinds and degrees from white to black; these two, as a rule, being particularly happy ones. If the ground stuff is patterned, as in

46

the case of a damasked silk, it must be specially chosen to suit the work to be placed upon it; small diaper patterns are frequently very good, since they break up the surface pleasantly without being too evident.

Linen, which well answers all the usual requirements, is, for this reason, very frequently chosen for a ground material. It can be procured in great variety, the hand-made linens being the best of all. Of kinds besides the ordinary are twilled linens, of which one named Kirriemuir twill is similar to the material used in the fine old embroidered curtains. Some damask linens look very well as backgrounds for embroidery; the pattern is sometimes a slightly raised diaper, which forms a pleasantly broken surface. Loosely woven linens can be obtained specially suitable for drawn thread work. In any case, if there is dressing in the new material, it must be well boiled before the embroidery is commenced : this makes it much softer for stitching through. Coloured linens are rarely satisfactory, a certain kind of blue being almost the only exception. The safest plan is to keep to pure white, or to the unbleached

47

varieties that have a slightly grey or warm tone about them. Wools, silks, and flax threads all look well upon a linen ground; it is not usually in good taste to embroider with poor thread upon a rich ground material, and, upon the other hand, gold thread and floss demand silk or velvet rather than linen, though any rule of this kind may on occasion be broken.

Velvet and satin make excellent backgrounds for rich work; they should not be used unless of good quality. The pile of the best velvet is shorter than that of poorer kinds, and so is easier to manipulate, which is a further reason for using the best. It is in any case a difficult material, so much so that work is often carried out on linen and afterwards applied to a velvet ground. The modern velvets, even the best of them, are for quality or colour not comparable with the old ones.

Silk of different kinds is largely employed, since it makes a suitable ground for many kinds of embroidery. Twilled and damasked silks are much used; in the last-named kind, patterns must be carefully chosen to suit the particular purpose. A thick ribbed silk is rarely satisfactory for embroidery purposes.

For working with silk thread, an untwisted floss takes the first place, but it needs some skill in manipulation. Filofloss is somewhat similar, but it has a slight twist in it, making it easier to work, though producing a less satisfactory result. Filosel is useful for some kinds of work, but it is a poorer quality of silk. The purse silks, and what is called embroidery silk, are all excellent; they are tightly twisted varieties of fine quality. There are various others in use; a visit to a good embroidery depôt will probably be the best means of finding out about these and about materials in general.

Wools can be obtained in various thicknesses and twistings, each good in their way. Some workers prefer a but slightly twisted wool; however, examples of old wool work are to be found in which a finely twisted variety is used with most satisfactory effect.

Flax threads can be obtained in very good colours, and are to be highly recommended. There are various cottons procurable, either coloured or white, that are good for marking and other embroidery

49

purposes where an evenly twisted thread is desirable.

Pearls and precious stones take their place in rich embroideries, also various less expensive but pretty stones may often be made use of effectively.

Beads are a fascinating material to work with; all kinds of pretty things can be done with them, either sewing them upon a ground, knitting or crocheting, or making use of a small bead loom. A good deal of the ready-made bought bead work, that only requires a monotonous ground to be filled in around an already worked pattern of sorts, is not at all suggestive of its possibilities. Beads of both paste and glass can be obtained in much greater variety than is usually known, from the most minute in size to large varieties of all kinds of shapes and patterns, the colours of most of them being particularly good. The larger ornamental beads are useful in many ways, sometimes taking the place of tassels or fringes.

Many kinds of most curious materials are at times brought into the service of embroidery, but the above-mentioned ones are the most usual.

CHAPTER III

PATTERN DESIGNING

The Difficulties of Pattern Making—A Stock-in-
Trade—Some Principles upon which Patterns
are Built Up—Spacing-Out—Nature and Convention—Shading—Figure Work—Limitations
—Colour.

A BEGINNER sometimes experiences difficulty in preparing her own patterns. A
designer needs a wide knowledge of many
subjects, which necessitates much time
being given to study; also drawing ability
is necessary to enable the worker to set
down her ideas upon paper. For much
simple and pretty work, however, a slight
acquaintance with drawing and design is
sufficient, and any one who can master the
requisite stitches can also acquire some
knowledge of these two subjects.

The word design frightens some who
do not know quite what it means or entails. Perhaps they do not realise that the
design has already been begun when the
object to be worked has been settled, and

51

the material, thread, and stitches have been decided upon—the rest comes in much the same way, partly by a system of choice; as it is necessary to know what materials there are which can be used, so must the chief varieties of pattern be known from which choice can be made. All patterns are built up on some fundamental plan, of which the number is comparatively small. The ability to choose, plan, and arrange is in a greater or less degree inherent in every one, so there should be, after all, no great difficulty in the design. The necessary underlying qualities are— a nice taste, freedom from affectation, an eye for colour and form, and, it might be added, a fair share of common sense.

A pattern maker requires some stock-in-trade, and it is wise to collect together a store of some well-classified design material of ascertained value, ready to be drawn upon when required. A good knowledge of plants and flowers is very necessary. This is best acquired by making careful drawings from nature. In choosing flowers for embroidery purposes, the best-known ones, such as the daisy, rose, or carnation, give more pleasure to the observer than rare unrecognisable varieties.

Figures, birds, beasts, and such things as inscriptions, monograms, shields of arms and emblems, all demand study and drawing, both from miscellaneous examples and from embroideries.

The treatment of all these should be studied in old work, in order that the curious conventions and all kinds of amusing and interesting ideas that have gradually grown up in the past may still be made use of and added to, instead of being cast aside in a wild endeavour after something original. The student who collects a supply of the foregoing materials will find she has considerably widened her knowledge during the process, and is better prepared to make designs.

In making a pattern the first thing to be decided upon is some main idea, the detail that is to carry it out must then be considered. This latter may be of various types, such as flowers, foliage, figures, animals, geometrical forms, interlacing strapwork, quatrefoils, &c., &c.; perhaps several of these *motifs* may be combined together in the same design.

One of the simplest plans upon which a pattern can be arranged is that of some form recurring at regular intervals over

FIG. 10.

the surface. The principle involved is repetition; an example of it is shown at fig. 10. The form that is used here is a sprig of flower, but the repeating element

FIG. 11

admits of infinite variation, it may be anything from a dot to an angel.

Copes and chasubles, bedspreads and curtains, are often to be seen decorated with some repeating form. Fig. 11

shows in outline a conventional sprig
that is repeated in this fashion over the
surface of a famous cope in Ely Cathedral.
Fig. 12 is an example of a sprig of flower
taken from a XVIIth century embroidered
curtain; similar bunches, but composed of
different flowers, recur at intervals over
this hanging.

It may interest the practical worker
to know what are the different stitches
used upon this figure. The petals of
the top flower are in chain stitch in
gradated colouring, the centre is an
open crossing of chain surrounded by
stamens in stem stitch in varied colour,
the outermost leaves are outlined in stem
stitch with an open filling of little crossed
stitches. The petals of the lower flower
are worked similarly, and the centre is
carried out in chain stitch and French
knots. The leaves are filled in with
ingenious variations of these stitches.

The repeating element is perhaps a
symbolical figure, a heraldic shield, or it
may be some geometrical form that sup-
plies the motive. Fig. 13 is a conventional
sprig of hawthorn that ornaments in this
way an altar frontal at Zanthen. It is
by no means necessary that the element

FIG. 12.

57

which repeats should be always identical;
so long as it is similar in size, form,
and general character it will probably be
the more interesting if variety is introduced.

The principle of repetition is again found
in fig. 14, but with an additional feature;

a sprig of flower is used,
with the further intro-
duction of diagonal lines,
expressed by leaf sprays,
which are arranged so as
to surround each flower
and divide it from the
adjoining ones.

It is advisable to space
out the required surface
in some way before com-
mencing to draw out a
pattern; for carrying out

FIG. 13.

fig. 14 it would be well to pencil out
the surface as in fig. 15; a connection
between these two will be perceived at a
glance. This spacing-out of the required
surface in one way or another is of great
assistance, and may even prove suggestive in
the planning of the design. It helps the
regularity of the work, and order is essential
in design as in most other things in life.

58

FIG. 14.

Another very usual expedient is that of introducing a main central form, with others branching out on either side and symmetrically balancing each other. An example of this is given in fig. 16. The symmetry may be much more free than this; a tree is symmetrical taken as a whole, but the two sides do not exactly repeat each other.

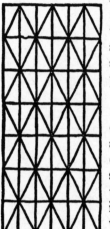

FIG. 15.

A plan very commonly employed is that of radiating main lines all diverging from one central point. Fig. 17 shows a design following this principle; there is infinite variety in the ways in which this may be carried out.

Another method would be to plan a continuous flowing line with forms branching out on one side or on both. Figs. 18 and 19 are border designs, for which purpose this arrangement is often used, though it can also well form an all-over pattern; sometimes these lines used over a surface are made to cross each

60

FIG. 16.

FIG. 17.

62

Figs. 18 and 19.   63

other, tartan wise, by running in two directions, producing an apparently complicated design by very simple means.

Designs may be planned on the counterchange principle. This is a system of mass designing that involves the problem of making a pattern out of one shape, continually repeated, and fitting into itself in such a way as to leave no interstices. The simplest example of this is to be found in the chess board, and it will easily be seen that a great number of shapes might be used instead of the square. Fig. 20 is

FIG. 20.

an example of a counterchange design carried out in inlay; for this method of work counterchange is very suitable. On reference to the chapter upon this work

64

another example will be found (page 181).
Fig. 21 illustrates the same principle, further complicated by the repetition of the form in three directions instead of in two only.

A method of further enriching a straightforward pattern, covering a plain

FIG. 21.

surface, is to work a subsidiary pattern upon the background. This is usually of a monotonous and formal character in order not to clash with the primary decoration, though this relationship may sometimes be found reversed. It has the appearance of being some decoration belonging to the ground rather than to the

primary pattern; in its simplest form it
appears as a mere repeating dot or a lattice
(see fig. 22), but it may be so elabo-
rated as to cover with an intricate design
every portion of the exposed ground not
decorated with the main pattern.

Many other distinct kinds of work
might be mentioned, such as needlework
pictures, the story-telling embroideries that
can be made so particularly attractive.
Embroidered landscapes, formal gardens,
mysterious woods, views of towns and
palaces, are, if rightly treated, very fine.
In order to learn the way to work such
subjects we must go to the XVIth and
XVIIth century *petit point* pictures, and
to the detail in fine tapestries. The
wrong method of going to work is to
imitate the effect sought after by the
painter.

It is a mistake in embroidery design
to be too naturalistic. In painting it
may be the especial aim to exactly imitate
nature, but here are wanted embroidery
flowers, animals and figures, possessing
the character and likeness of the things
represented, but in no way trying to make
us believe that they are real. The sem-
blance of a bumble bee crawling upon the

66

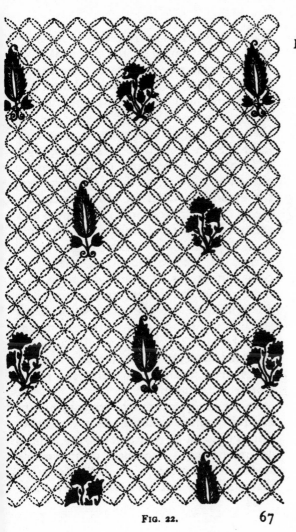

FIG. 22.

tea cloth gives a hardly pleasant sensation and much savours of the practical joke, which is seldom in good taste; the needle, however, adds convention to almost anything, and will usually manage the bee all right unless the worker goes out of the way to add a shadow and a high light. Such things as perspective, light and shade or modelling of form, should all be very much simplified if not avoided, for embroidery conforms to the requirements of decoration and must not falsify the surface that it ornaments. Shading is made use of in order to give more variety to, and exhibit the beauty of, colour by means of gradation, to explain more clearly the design, and so on; it is not employed for the purpose of fixing the lighting of the composition from one point by means of systematically adjusted light and shade, or of making a form stand out so realistically as to almost project from the background.

In avoiding too much resemblance to natural forms it is not necessary to make things ugly; a conventional flower implies no unmeaning straightness or impossible curve, it may keep all its interesting characteristics, but it has to obey other

68

requirements specially necessary in the particular design. Another point to be noted is that, since there is freedom of choice of flowers and other objects, only those perfect and well-formed should be chosen; all accidents of growth and disease may, happily, be omitted; if anything of this kind is put in it helps to give the naturalistic look which is to be avoided. Both sides of a leaf should match, though it may happen in nature, through misfortune, that one is deformed and small.

In figure work, which, though ambitious, is one of the most interesting kinds of embroidery, the figures, like all other things, must be treated with a certain amount of simplicity; very little attempt must be made to obtain flesh tones, roundness of form, perspective, or foreshortening. The work should be just sufficiently near to nature to be a good embroidery rendering of it. However, without overstepping the limits there is a great deal that may be expressed, such things as character, gesture, grace, colour, and so on, matters which are after all of first importance. Detail, if of the right kind, may be filled in, but it is wrong to attempt what is to the craft

69

very laborious to obtain, for this would be
misdirected energy, which is great waste.
A right use of the figure can be seen in
the XIIIth century embroidery pictures,
which, covering mediæval church vestments, often display episodes from the
lives of the saints. These are some of the
masterpieces of the art of embroidery;
observation of nature is carried to a marvellous pitch, but the execution never
sinks into commonplace realism.

Certain restrictions are always present,
in making a design, that must be con-
formed to, such as, the limit of space,
the materials with which the work is to
be carried out, the use to which it will be
put, and so on. These, instead of being
difficulties, can afford help in the way of
suggestion and limitation. A bad design
may look as if it obeyed them unwillingly
—a form is perhaps cramped, perhaps
stretched out in order to fit its place,
instead of looking as if it naturally fitted
it whether the confining lines were there
or not. In the early herbals, illustrated
with woodcuts, examples can be found
over and over again of a flower filling a
required space simply and well; fig. 23 is
taken from the herbal of Carolus Clusius,

Fig. 23.

printed at Antwerp in 1601 by the great
house of Plantin. The draughtsman in this
case had to draw a plant to fit a standard-
sized engraver's block, and he had a certain
number of facts to tell about it; he drew
the plant as simply and straightforwardly as
possible, making good use of all the available space, the result being a well-planned
and balanced piece of work, with no affectation or unnecessary lines about it.

Fine colour is a quality appreciated at
first sight, though often unconsciously.
It is a difficult subject to speak of very
definitely; an eye for colour is natural to
some, but in any case the faculty can be
cultivated and developed. By way of
studying the subject, we can go to nature
and learn as much as we are capable of
appreciating; even such things as butter-
flies, shells, and birds' eggs are suggestive.
Again, embroideries, illuminated manuscripts, pictures, painted decoration, may
be studied, and so on; in fact, colour is
so universal that it is not possible to get
away from it. Unfortunately we are
sometimes forced to learn what to avoid
as well as what to emulate.

Colour is entirely relative, that is to
say it depends upon its immediate sur-

roundings for what it appears to be. Also it has effects varying with the material which it dyes; wool is of an absorbent nature, whereas silk has powers of reflection. It is a safe plan to use true colours, real blue, red or green, not slate, terra cotta, and olive. Gold, silver, white and black, are valuable additions to the colour palette; it should be remembered about the former that precious things must be used with economy or they become cheap and perhaps vulgar.

For getting

FIG. 24.

73

satisfactory colour there is a useful method
which can at times be made use of;
this is to stitch it down in alternate
lines of two different tints, which, seen
together at a little distance, give the
desired effect. Backgrounds can be
covered over with some small geometrical pattern carried out in this way,
such as is shown in fig. 24, perhaps using
in alternation bright blue and black instead of a single medium tint of blue all
over. At a slight distance the tone may
be the same in either case, but this
method gives a pleasantly varied and refined effect, which avoids muddiness, and
shows up the pattern better. This same
method is used for expressing form more
clearly as well as for colour; waves of
hair, for instance, are much more clearly
expressed when worked in this way.

74

CHAPTER IV

STITCHES

IT is necessary for every worker to have a certain amount of knowledge of stitches, for they are, so to speak, the language of the art, and though not of first importance, still there is a great deal in stitchery. The needlewoman should be absolute master of her needle, for there is a great charm in beautifully carried out stitching; also a good design can be made mechanical and uninteresting by a wrong method of execution. The simplest and most common stitches are the best, and are all that are necessary for the doing of good work. Work carried out entirely in one stitch has a certain unity and character that is very pleasing. There are a great number of stitches in existence, that is, if each slight

75

variation has a different name assigned to it. The names are sometimes misleading, for often the same stitch is known by several different ones; descriptive names have where possible been chosen for those discussed in the following pages.

A worker may find it useful to keep by her a sampler with the most characteristic stitches placed upon it; a glance at this will be suggestive when she is in doubt as to which to use, for it is often difficult to recollect just the right and most suitable one at a moment's notice. It is necessary to learn only the main varieties, for each individual worker can adapt, combine, and invent variations to suit a special purpose.

The direction of the stitch is important; tone, if not colour, can be very much altered by change in direction; also growth and form can be suggested by it; for instance, lines going across a stem are not usually so satisfactory as those running the length of it; these suggesting growth better. Folds of drapery are often explained by direction of the lines of stitching quite as much as by gradation of colour.

76

With reference to the stitches described in the following chapters, the worker is advised to try to work them by simply examining the diagrams, and, if in any difficulty, then to refer to the printed description, for such directions are apt to be tedious. The simplest way to master these is to let some one read them out step by step, and to work from dictation. It should be remembered that the use of a particular thread often makes or mars a stitch, some requiring soft silks to show them to advantage, whilst others may need a stoutly twisted thread.

Chain stitch is universal, and one of the most ancient of stitches. It is the most commonly used of a group that might be described as linked stitches. Much beautiful work has been carried out entirely in it, and when a monotonous even line is required, this is a most suitable stitch to employ. It is equally in request for outline and filling in, and its chain - like adaptability makes it specially good for following out curved forms or spiral lines. Tambour stitch is practically the same in result, though worked in quite a different manner, for it is carried out in a frame with a fine

77

crochet hook, instead of with a needle. This makes it quicker in execution, but more mechanical in appearance, so it is not to be as much recommended.

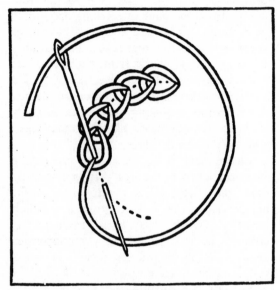

FIG. 25.

To work chain stitch (fig. 25) bring the needle through at the top of the traced line, hold the working thread down towards the left with the thumb, insert the needle at the point where the

78

thread has just come through and bring it up on the traced line about one-sixteenth of an inch further along, draw the thread through over the held down thread. It should show a neat line of back-stitching on the reverse side. The chain can be made broader by inserting the needle a little to the right, instead of at the exact point where the last thread came through. Care must be taken in the working not to draw the thread too tightly, as this stitch is inclined to pucker the material, especially when it is worked in curved lines.

A flower and leaf worked with a solid filling of chain stitch are shown in fig. 26. The dark outline of the flower is in back stitch, the centre a mass of French knots, and the stem in stem stitch. By working the petals in curved lines in this way the shape is well suggested, and the play of light on the curves is particularly happy, especially if the thread used is silk or gold. Another slight variation from this would be to work the lines of chain stitch in different shades of colour, and so get each petal gradually either lighter or darker towards its base; this gives a very pretty effect. Fig. 27 shows an oak leaf

79

Stitches carried out in this way, the lines upon it

Fig. 26.

indicate the way in which the stitches
80

would be worked. The rule in solid fillings is to work from the outside inwards where possible, and thus make sure of a good outline.

In the Victoria and Albert Museum there is a white linen dress[1] daintily embroidered in chain stitch. It is an excellent example of a kind of design suitable to this stitch; the leaves and flowers are carried out in lines of chain stitch following the outline, and in these lines use is made of strongly contrasting colour to both show up the form

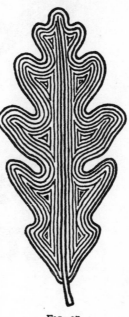

FIG. 27.

better, and also decorate it. The leaf in fig. 28 is in style somewhat similar to this, and is intended to be carried out in two distinct colours.

[1] No. 184, 1898.

81

FIG. 28.

Chain stitches can be worked singly; they are used in this way as a powdering over a background. Sometimes they may be seen conventionally suggesting the small feathers on the shoulder of a bird's wing by being dotted over it at regular intervals. Fig. 29 shows how they might be used to carry out a tiny flower, five separate stitches represent the petals, and two more the leaves at the base; this is a simpler and more satisfactory method than to attempt very minute forms with satin stitches.

FIG. 29.

The common chain makes a particularly neat border stitch taken in zigzag fashion. To work this (fig. 30)—Trace two parallel lines on the material and work the chain across from side to side at an angle of 45° to the traced lines. For further security it is well to catch down the end of the stitch just completed with the needle as it commences the following

83

one. The line can be further decorated by placing a French knot, perhaps in a contrasting colour, in each little triangular space left by working the stitch.

FIG. 30.

There is an ingenious method of working ordinary chain stitch in a chequering of two colours (fig. 31). It is quite

FIG. 31.

simple to work. Thread a needle with two different coloured threads, commence the chain stitch in the usual way

84

until the thread has to be placed under the point of the needle for forming the loop. Place only one of the two threads underneath, leaving the other on one side out of the way, then draw the needle and thread through over the one held down. A chain stitch will have been formed with the thread that was looped under the needle. For the next stitch, the alternate thread is placed under, and so on, taking each thread in turn. The thread not in use each time usually requires a little adjustment to make it entirely disappear from the surface.

Twisted chain is worked very similarly to the ordinary chain stitch. It has not such a decidedly looped appearance, which is sometimes an advantage. To work it (fig. 32)—Bring the thread through at the top of the line, hold it down under the thumb to the left, and insert the needle to the left of the traced line, slightly below the point where the thread has come through. Bring it out again on the traced line, about one-eighth of an inch lower down, and draw it through over the held down thread.

An entirely different effect can be obtained by working this stitch much

85

closer together, but in exactly the same way. It will then resemble a satin stitch slightly raised on one side. This is

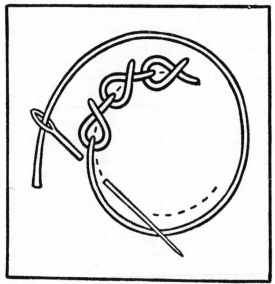

FIG. 32.

known as rope stitch and is at times very useful.

Open chain stitch makes a good broad line; it looks best when worked with a stout thread. To carry out the stitch (fig. 33)—Trace two parallel lines upon the material, about one-eighth of an inch apart, and bring the thread through at the top of the left-hand one. Hold the

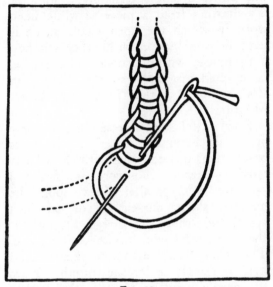

FIG. 33.

thread down with the thumb and insert the needle exactly opposite on the other line, bring it up one-eighth of an inch lower down and draw the thread through over the held down part, leaving a rather slack loop upon the material.

87

Then insert the needle on the first line again, inside the slack loop, and bring it out one-eighth of an inch below. Repeat this on each side alternately. Fig. 34 is a drawing from a piece of white linen work in which the open chain stitch is used in combination with other stitches. This figure, with its open-work centre, is repeated diagonally over a white linen cloth exhibited in the Victoria and Albert Museum.

Braid stitch rather resembles a fancy braid laid upon the material. It looks best when carried out with a stoutly twisted thread. To work it (fig. 35) —Trace two parallel lines upon the material about one-eighth of an inch apart, and bring the thread through at the right-hand end of the lower line. Throw the thread across to the left and hold it slackly under the thumb. Place the needle pointing towards the worker under this held thread, then twist it round towards the left and over the held thread until it points in the opposite direction. It will now have the thread twisted loosely over it. Next, insert the needle on the upper line one-eighth of an inch from the starting-point, and bring it

FIG. 34.

89

through on the lower line exactly underneath. Place the thumb over the stitch in process of making and draw the thread through as the diagram shows. It can

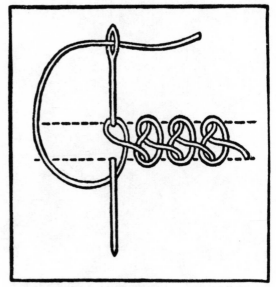

FIG. 35.

be worked openly or more closely as preferred.

Cable chain is descriptively named, for, when worked with a stoutly twisted thread, it has very much the appearance of a chain laid upon the material, rather too much so perhaps to be a pretty embroidery stitch. To work it (fig. 36)— Bring the needle through at the top of the

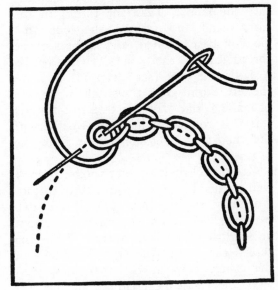

FIG. 36.

traced line, throw the thread round to the left and hold it down with the thumb near where it has come through the material. Pass the needle under the held down thread from left to right and draw it

91

through until there is only a small loop left.
Insert the needle in the centre of this loop,
on the traced line about one-sixteenth of
an inch below the starting-point. Bring
it out a quarter of an inch below and outside the loop. Take the thread in the
right hand and tighten the loop that
has now been formed, and then pass the
thread under the point of the needle
towards the left (see diagram). Place
the left thumb over the stitch in process
of making and draw the thread through;
this will complete the first two links of
the chain; to continue, repeat from the
beginning.

Knotted chain is a pretty stitch; to look
well it must be worked with a stout thread.
To carry it out (fig. 37)—Trace two
parallel lines upon the material, about
one-eighth of an inch apart. Bring the
thread through at the right hand end in
the centre between the two lines, then
insert the needle on the upper line one-sixteenth of an inch further along, and bring
it through on the lower line immediately
below. Draw the thread through and
there will be a short slanting line left
upon the material. Throw the thread
round to the left and hold it under the

92

thumb, then pass the needle and thread
through the slanting line from above
downwards, leaving the thread a little
slack. Place the thread again under

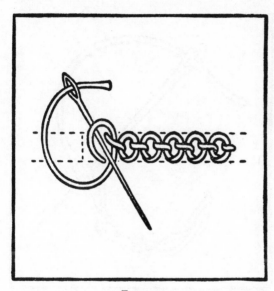

FIG. 37.

the thumb, then in the same way as
before, from above downwards, pass the
needle and thread through this slack loop.
This makes the first two links of the
chain; the last one will not be properly

93

fixed in place until the next stitch is taken. The dotted vertical line on the diagram shows the piece of material taken up by the needle upon commencing the next stitch.

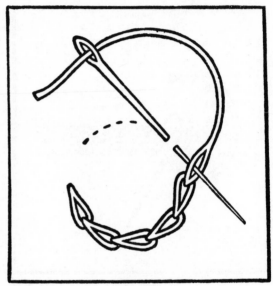

FIG. 38.

Split stitch is a most useful one for many purposes. It is difficult to distinguish from a fine chain when done, but in the working it much more resembles stem stitch. It can be carried out ın the hand or in a frame. This stitch, frequently seen upon ancient work, was much used for both draperies and features; the lines of the stitching usually, by their direction, expressing moulding of form or folds of drapery. To work it (fig. 38) —Bring the thread through at the lower end of the traced line, then insert the needle about one-eighth of an inch further along, and bring it through on the line two or three threads nearer the starting-point; whilst bringing it through take it also through the centre of the working thread, which thus splits each stitch.

CHAPTER V

STITCHES—(*continued*)

SATIN AND SIMILAR STITCHES

SATIN stitch is perhaps the most commonly used of all stitches. It is more

95

quickly worked by hand, but for complicated
work the help of a frame is required.
Floss silk thread is seen to greatest advantage in a stitch of this kind, for it shows off

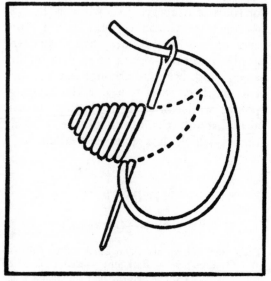

FIG. 39.

the glossiness of silk particularly well. It
is straightforward in the working and needs
no further description than is given by the
diagram (fig. 39). The stitches may vary
in length, they must neither be impracti-

96

cably long nor, on the other hand, too much cut up, lest the silky effect be partly lost. These stitches lie close together and in parallel lines; the chief difference between satin and several other closely allied stitches being that these others may radiate or vary in direction according to the space to be filled. The stitch is usually worked in oblique lines; stems, leaves, and petals would be treated in this way; sometimes it is worked regularly having regard to the warp and woof of the material; it would be treated thus when used in conjunction with cross or stroke stitch.

It will be seen that there is as much silk at the back as on the front of the work. There is a method of carrying out the stitch by which this waste of material at the back is avoided; the thread is returned to the front close to where it went through instead of crossing over and coming up on the other side. The effect on the right side, however, is not so good, so this method cannot be recommended.

One of the technical difficulties with satin stitch is to get a neat firm line at the edges of the filled space; this is excellently attained by the Chinese and Japanese, who use this satin stitch a great

97

deal. They frequently work each petal of a complicated flower separately, leaving as a division, between each one and the next, a fine line of material firmly and clearly drawn.

The stitch is much used for raised work, and also lends itself well to gradation of colour. Fig. 40 is an example of shading in satin stitch. In this case each new row of stitches fits in just between those of the last row; this is a bold but very effective method of expressing gradation. A variation upon this is shown in fig. 42 ; the bands of different colour are here necessarily worked in a chevron pattern which makes the shading rather more

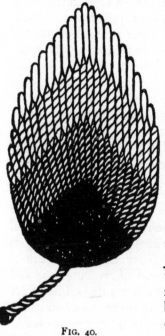

FIG. 40.

gradual. An example of the same thing can be seen in fig. 44 in the leaf upon which the squirrel sits. Apart from gradation of colour, the surface to be covered by satin stitch has often to be partitioned

FIG. 41.

up in some way in order to make the satin stitches of a practical length.

Long and short stitch is a very slight variation, if any, from satin stitch. The name describes the method of working, for it is carried out by working alternately a long and a short stitch, the stitches being

99

picked up just as in satin stitch. It is useful for close fillings and shaded work, and also as a solid outline for any kind of open filling. The working of the stitch

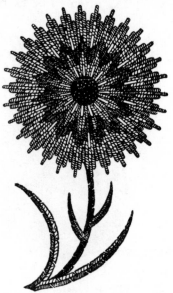

FIG. 42.

can be seen in fig. 41, where the band of lightest colour on the upper part of the leaf is worked in long and short stitch. The advantage of this way of working can be seen at once, it makes a firm outline on the one edge and a nicely broken-

up one on the other, just ready for
another shade to be worked in. In order
to carry out the rest of the shading on
the leaf in the same way the stitches can
be all of the same length; this will always
ensure a broken line at the edge, which is
a necessity for this method of gradation.
Long and short stitch used as an outline for
a leaf with an open filling can be seen on
page 209. The *opus plumarium* or feather
stitch that we read of in the descriptions of
the old embroideries was a similar stitch
to this, and so called, some say, because
it resembled the plumage of a bird.

Stem stitch, well known and frequently
in use for various purposes, such as for
lines, outlines, gradated and flat fillings, and
so on, is usually done in the hand, and is
quite simple; fig. 43 explains the working.
If a broad line is required the needle is
put in more obliquely, and a raised effect
can be obtained by working over a laid
thread. The thread must be kept to the
same side of the needle, either to the left or
to the right as better suits the purpose in
hand; the effect is more line-like when it
is kept to the right. Occasionally, when
just a double line is to be worked, it is
deliberately done in the two ways, and

101

then the line resembles **a** narrow plait. A solid filling in stem stitch should be worked in lines as illustrated in the squirrel in fig. 44. This little beast is

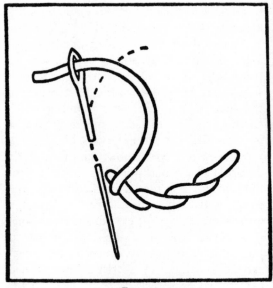

FIG. 43.

taken from the curtain shown in Plate VII., and is a good example of the life and interest that the introduction of such things adds to embroideries.

The stitches just described were largely

102

used in crewel work. This is a rather

FIG. 44.

vague name that denotes a decorative kind

FIG. 45.

of needlework carried out with coloured wools upon a plain white linen ground. The design is usually composed of conventionally treated leaves and flowers, often

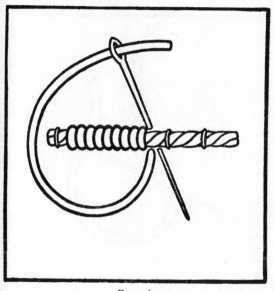

FIG. 46.

growing from boldly curved stems. These were partly shaded in solid stitches, partly worked with geometrical open fillings; ornamental birds and beasts of all kinds were introduced, and the effect of the whole was very beautiful. The work is

105

characteristically English, and a great deal of it was executed in the XVIIth century. Plates VII. and VIII. are illustrative of the type of work, and fig. 45 represents a

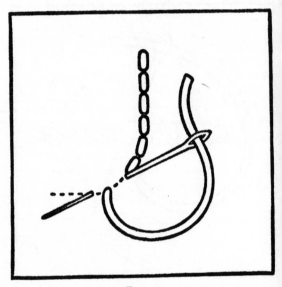

FIG. 47.

detail. The various stitches which occur in this drawing are stem, herring-bone, long and short, knot, basket, buttonhole, single chain and satin stitches.

Overcast stitch in embroidery is practically a very short raised satin stitch. It requires neat workmanship, and then makes a bold clear line or outline. To work it (fig. 46)—Run or couch down a thread on the traced line, then with fine thread cover this over with close upright stitches, picking up as little material as possible each time in order to make the line clear and round. The stitch is worked most perfectly in a frame.

Back stitch sometimes makes a good line or outline. To work it (fig. 47)—Bring the needle through one-sixteenth of an inch from the end of the traced line, insert it at the commencement and bring it through again one-sixteenth of an inch beyond where it first came out. Each stitch, it will be seen, commences at the point where the last one finished.

BUTTONHOLE STITCH AND ITS APPLICATION

Buttonhole stitch, which is well known in plain needlework, is very useful also in embroidery, besides being an important stitch in needlepoint lace. Owing to its construction it is well suited for the covering of raw edges, but it is also adaptable to a variety of other purposes, such as are open or close fillings of leaves and flowers, cut work, and the outlining of applied work.

There are two ways of forming the

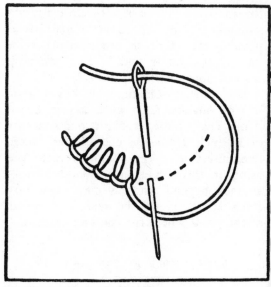

Fig. 48.

stitch, the common buttonhole and what is called tailor's buttonhole.

To work the ordinary buttonhole stitch (fig. 48)—Bring the needle through at the left-hand end of the traced line, hold

108

the thread down to the left with the
thumb and insert the needle as shown in
the diagram, draw it through over the
held thread to complete the stitch. It

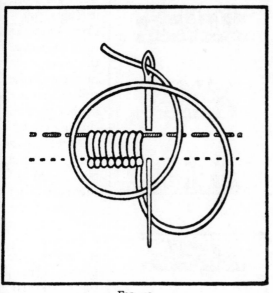

Fig. 49.

is worked openly in the diagram, but
it may, as required, be either more or less
open or quite closed.

The tailor's buttonhole is for some
purposes more satisfactory; the stitch is

firmer than the other kind owing to the heading having an extra knot in it; this makes it also more ornamental. To work it (fig. 49)— Commence in the same way as the last stitch until the needle and thread are in the position shown in fig. 48 then, with the right hand take hold of the thread near the eye of the needle, bring it down and loop it under the point from right to left, draw the needle and thread

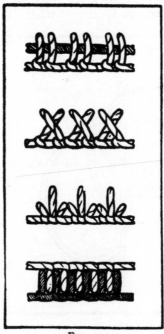

FIG. 50

through over these two loops, and the first stitch is made.

Buttonhole stitch can be varied in many ways, dependent mainly upon the spacing

110

of the stitch and the direction that the needle takes when picking up the material. Fig. 50 shows four simple varieties; the first is the open buttonhole spaced slightly

FIG. 51.

irregularly and with a thread slipped underneath it; any variety of spacing can be arranged, and the thread shown running underneath, which sometimes forms a pretty addition, is usually of a contrasting colour or material. The second

III

shows the stitches taken slanting-wise, so that they cross each other. In the third the stitches are at different angles and of unequal length. The fourth example shows two lines of spaced buttonhole stitch fitting neatly the one into the other and forming a solid line. One row is worked first, leaving just sufficient space between each stitch for the second row to fill up, which can be carried out by reversing the position of the material and exactly repeating the first line in the same or in a different colour.

A flower filled in with open buttonhole stitch is shown at fig. 51. The centre consists of a mass of French knots, and the outside line is in satin stitch. The innermost circle of buttonholing is worked first, the next row is worked over the heading of the first row as well as into the material; the succeeding rows are worked in the same way until the outside limit is reached, and there the satin stitch just covers the heading of the last row of buttonhole stitching. Gradation of colour can easily be introduced by using a different shade for each circle of stitches, and this produces a very pretty effect. An open method of filling a

space, whether flower, leaf, drapery, or
background, is sometimes preferable to a
solid filling, and the two methods can

FIG. 52.

very well be used together as each shows
off the other. These light fillings give
opportunity for further variety and ingenuity in the stitching, and prevent the
work from looking heavy. A butterfly,

113

carried out partly in open stitches, is illustrated in fig. 52.

Fig. 53 is, in the original, a gay little flower carried out in orange and yellow. The stitch employed here is a close buttonhole.

Another example of the use of close

FIG. 53.

buttonhole is shown in the ivy leaf in fig. 54. The stitch is worked in two rows, back to back, in each lobe of the leaf, and the resulting ridge down the centre rather happily suggests the veining. This method of filling in might be just reversed for a rose leaf; the heading of

114

the stitch would then suggest the serrated edge, and the meeting of the two rows down the centre the line of the vein.

A cluster of berries can be very prettily worked in buttonhole stitch in the way shown in fig. 55. The stitches are so

FIG. 54.

arranged that the heading outlines each berry, and the needle enters the material at the same point, always in the centre. A bullion stitch in a darker colour marks the eye of the berry.

A good method of filling a space with solid buttonhole stitching is shown in

FIG. 55.

116

fig. 56. Each row is worked into the heading of the preceding row, and the stitches do not pierce the material except

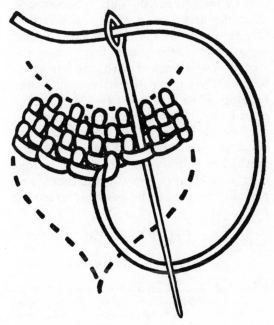

FIG. 56.

in the first row and at the extremities of succeeding rows. They are placed rather close together in order to completely cover the ground. The stitch is worked, first, from left to right, then for the next row from right to left; this is quite easy and enables the work to be continuously carried out. Sometimes, when the first row is done, the thread is thrown across to the side where the row began, and there made fast; then the second row is worked with stitches which take up the thrown thread as well as the heading of the first row. By using a more open buttonhole and thus partly exposing the laid thread, a filling, both quick and effective, is obtained. This is a useful method to employ when the work is done over a padding of threads, for there is no necessity to pierce the material except at the edges.

CHAPTER VI

STITCHES—(*continued*)

Knots and Knot Stitches—Herring-bone Stitch—
Feather Stitch—Basket Stitch—Fishbone Stitch
—Cretan Stitch—Roumanian Stitch—Various
Insertion Stitches—Picots.

KNOTS AND KNOT STITCHES

IT would be difficult to go far in embroidery without requiring knots for one purpose or another. They are useful in all sorts of ways, and make a pleasant contrast to the other stitches. For the enrichment of border lines and various parts of the work, both pattern and background, they are most serviceable, and also for solid fillings; for such places as centres of flowers or parts of leaves, they are again valuable. They have been used to form a continuous outline, but owing to their tendency to make a weak line, not frequently; indeed they usually show to better advantage when slightly separated.

Examples are to be seen of English knotted line work in which the knotting was executed in the thread previously to embroidering with it. The knotting of thread was a pastime with ladies in the XVIIth century. The thread, usually a linen one and as a rule home spun, was wound upon a netting-needle, and by the aid of this a close series of knots was made upon it; when finished it somewhat resembled a string of beads. Balls of this prepared knotted thread may still be found, treasured up in old work receptacles. When prepared it was couched on to the material with fine thread, like a cord or braid, and made to follow out some prearranged pattern.

119

In white linen work it was used for carrying out ornamental borderings on infants' robes and other dainty articles.

French knots can be worked in the

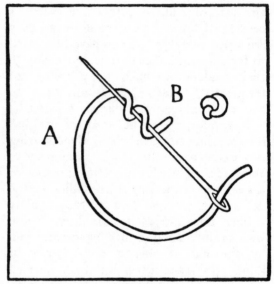

FIG. 57.

hand or in a frame. They are easier to manage in the latter, and to look well they must be neatly and firmly made. Completed they should resemble beads lying end upwards on the material. To work the French knot (fig. 57)—Bring the thread through the material at the required point, take hold of it with the left finger and thumb near the starting-point (A on plan), then let the point of the needle encircle the held thread twice, twist the needle round and insert it at point B on plan, draw the thread through to the back, not letting go the held thread until necessary. Fig. 58 shows some French knots decorating a leaf spray, and various other

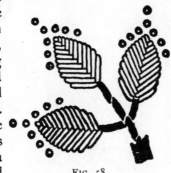

FIG. 58.

examples of their use can be found in the book.

Bullion knots resemble tight curls of thread laid on the material. They can be used as a variation from French knots, and even for the representation of petals and small leaves. To be satisfactory they must be firm, stout, and tightly coiled; some knack is required to make them properly.

To work the bullion knot (fig. 59)—
Bring the thread through at the required
place, insert the needle one-eighth of an
inch from this point and bring it through

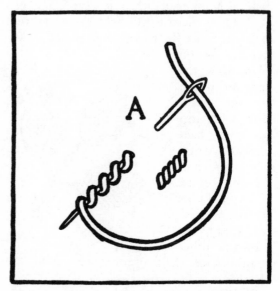

FIG. 59.

again exactly at it.　Take hold of the
thread about two inches from where it
came through and twist it several times
round the point of the needle, the number
of times being dependent on the required

122

length of the knot. Place the left thumb
upon the tight coil on the needle, in order
to keep it in place, and draw the needle
and thread through it, then pass the thread

FIG. 60.

through to the back at the point where
the needle was last inserted (point A on
plan). The thumb must not be removed
until it is in the way. Fig. 60 represents
a flower, of which the centre is formed of
bullion together with French knots.

123

Fig. 61 shows a knotted stitch that is similar in result to the knotted threads discussed earlier in the chapter. In this

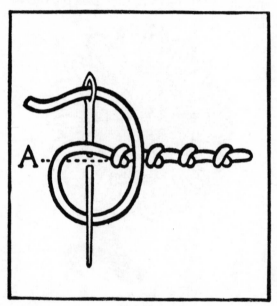

FIG. 61.

case the knotting of the thread and the fixing to the material is done at the same time. It is a useful stitch when a jagged line is wanted, and can be seen used, for instance, for the branching veins in open work leaves, as in fig. 62. The diagram explains the working of the stitch; at

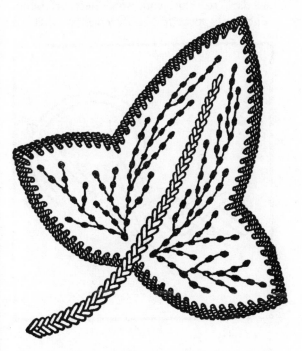

FIG. 62.

point A on the plan the left thumb holds the thread down whilst the stitch is in progress.

The stitch illustrated at fig. 63 is very
similar to the common herring-bone.
The only practical difference is that in

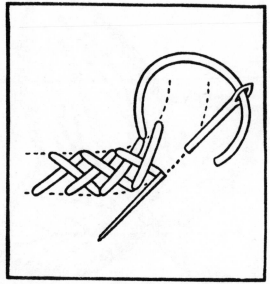

FIG. 63.

the plain needlework stitch there is usually
a smaller piece of material picked up by
the needle each time. To work it as in
the diagram—Trace two parallel lines on

126

the material and bring the thread through at the commencement of the lower line, insert it on the opposite line rather farther along and there pick up a stitch, as the needle is doing in the figure. Then on the opposite line pick up a similar stitch a little in advance of the one just finished. After this work the stitches on either line alternately, commencing each one at the point where the last one ended; this forms on the underside a double row of back stitches. It is quite easy to work this stitch with the back stitches on the working side, and when they are required to be on the surface it is advisable to do it in that way. When embroidering upon a semi-transparent material this stitch is a satisfactory one to use, the back stitching follows out the outline on either side of the form, and the crossing of the threads on the under side shows through prettily. This stitch sometimes goes by the name of double back stitch. It is useful in many ways, making a light stitch for stems, leaves, or flowers; it can be sometimes found in Eastern work used for an entire embroidery. When used for flowers or leaves the width and the closeness of the stitch

127

Stitches are varied to suit the shape to be filled. An example of its use as a flower filling is

FIG. 64.

shown in the carnation at fig. 64, which is carried out in four shades of colour. Considerable use is made of this stitch in

128

embroidered curtain shown in Plate VII. ;
it is there employed for all the stems and
various flowers upon the hanging.

The feather stitch, often used to deco-

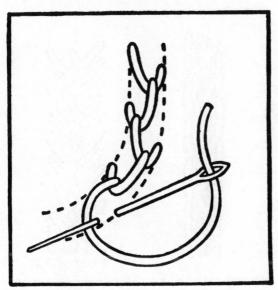

FIG. 65.

rate plain needlework, is now to be discussed ; although similar in name it must
not be confused with the feather or plumage
stitch that has already been mentioned.
The stitch is so simple and so much in

129

use as hardly to need description; fig. 65 explains the working. There can be many slight variations of the stitch, the worker perhaps devising them needle in hand.

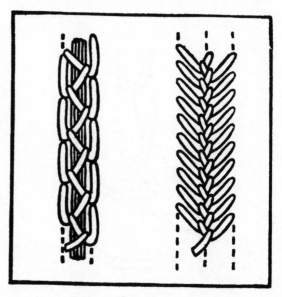

FIG. 66.

Two are shown in fig. 66. The one to the left is worked very like the ordinary stitch; the needle picks up the material in a straight line instead of slightly obliquely, and each stitch touches the one immediately above; it is here made use of as a couching stitch, a bunch of threads of a contrasting colour is laid on the material, and the stitch worked over it from side to side. The right-hand example shows the ordinary feather stitch worked more closely and in a broader line; carried out in this way, it can be used for a leaf filling.

Basket stitch, useful for a solid line, shows up very clearly when worked with a stout twisted thread. This stitch would be appropriately used when applied to some representation of basket work. To carry out the diagram (fig. 67)—Trace two parallel lines on the material, and to commence, bring the thread through on the left-hand line, then insert the needle on the right-hand line about one-eighth of an inch lower down and bring it through on the left-hand line exactly opposite (see needle in fig.); the next stitch is worked by inserting the needle on the right-hand line but above the last stitch, that is at point A on diagram, and bringing it through at B. To continue, repeat from the beginning.

A particularly good line for a border is made by fishbone stitch. It can be worked in one colour, or as easily in a

131

chequering of two or three, as shown in
the diagram (fig. 68); to carry it out in
this way the worker must have two threads
in use, bringing through each as required.

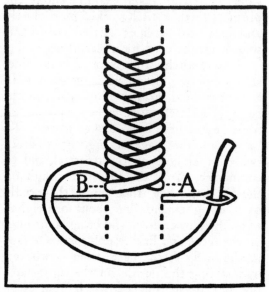

FIG. 67.

For such purposes as the fillings of small
leaves, this stitch is very useful (see fig. 58).
The meeting of the stitches in the centre
suggest the veining line, also the change
in direction of the thread gives, to the

two sides of the leaf, pleasant variation in tone. To work it—Trace three parallel lines upon the material and bring the thread through on the upper line at the

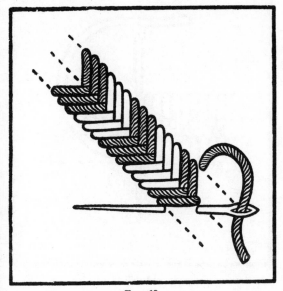

FIG. 68.

left-hand end. Insert the needle and bring it through as in process in the diagram, then repeat the same stitch on the other side the reverse way, that is, insert the needle just over the central line

133

and bring it through on the upper one close to the last stitch. Care must be taken that the stitches cross well over

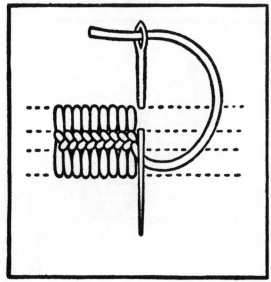

FIG. 69.

each other at the centre, or the material will show through.

The stitch shown in fig. 69, known as plait or Cretan, is commonly seen on Cretan and other Eastern embroideries. It can be used as a solid border stitch or

134

Fig. 70.

135

as a filling, varying in width as required. To work it—Bring the thread through on the lower central line, then insert the needle on the uppermost line and bring it through on the next below as in process in the diagram; then, still keeping the thread to the right, insert the needle immediately underneath on the lowest line and bring it through on the line next above, in fashion similar to the last stitch, but in reverse direction. To continue, work the stitch alternately on one side and the other, always keeping the thread to the right of the needle. In order to make the central plait broader take up rather less material with the needle; this will decrease the outer and increase the inner lines. Fig. 70 is taken from a Cretan embroidery, in which this stitch is mainly used.

Another similar but more simple stitch, often seen in Eastern work, is shown in fig. 71. It can also frequently be found employed on XVIIth century English wool work hangings. It is sometimes called Roumanian stitch, and is composed of one long stitch crossed by a short one in the centre. To work it—Trace two parallel lines on the material

and bring the thread through on the left-
hand line at the top. Insert the needle
on the opposite line and bring it through
near the centre, as shown in process in

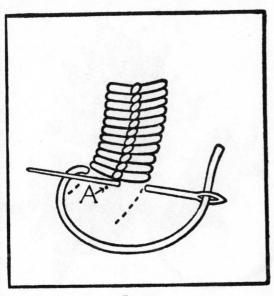

Fig. 71.

the diagram. For the next half of the
stitch the needle enters the material at
point A on plan, and is brought through
again on the left-hand line close to the
last stitch, and so in position to commence

137

again. An illustration of this stitch in use as a filling can be seen at fig. 72. It is worked in four shades of green wool,

FIG. 72.

and each line of stitches is so arranged as to encroach slightly on the line before by means of setting each stitch just between two of the last row. This method of working has two advantages; the shading

138

is thus made more gradual, and a pleasant
undulating effect is given to the surface
of the leaf. This can be most easily
understood by a practical trial of the stitch
and method.

INSERTION STITCHES

There is occasion sometimes in embroidery to join edges together visibly.
This gives an opportunity for some additional pretty stitching—the addition of
something like this, that is perhaps not
absolutely necessary, has extra value from
the evidence it gives of the worker's
interest and delight in her work, a
quality always appreciated; on the other
hand, work done from the motive of
getting a result with as little labour as
possible is valued at just its worth.

These insertion stitches are useful for
joining together edges of cushion covers,
bags, detached bands, also for the ornamentation of dress, and for embroideries
upon which drawn thread work is not
possible. A stout thread is usually suitable for the purpose. The raw edges
must first be turned in and flattened, and
the parts to be joined can if necessary be

tacked in place on a temporary ground such as *toile cirée*.

Fig. 73 illustrates a twisted insertion stitch that is quickly executed and very frequently used. The diagram sufficiently explains the working without further description.

Buttonhole stitch can be turned to

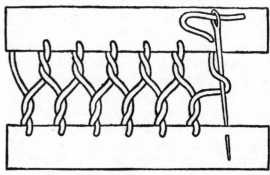

account for this purpose. Fig. 74 shows the tailor's buttonhole used as an insertion stitch; for this purpose it is the better of the two kinds of buttonhole. The stitches could be arranged in various ways; in the present example three are worked closely together on either side in turn. The only difficulty with this buttonhole insertion is that on one side the stitch has to be worked in direction contrary to that usual,

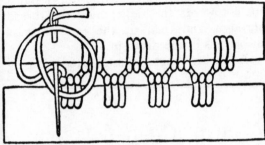

Fig. 74.

that is from right to left instead of from left to right. In the diagram the needle is shown working in this reverse way.

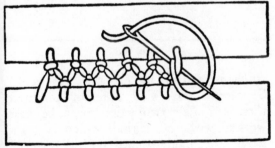

Fig. 75.

Fig. 75 is a knotted insertion stitch; the knot at each side makes the stitch a very rigid one. To work it—Bring the thread through at the lower left-hand side. insert the needle on the upper side a little towards the right, draw the thread through, and then tie the knot on it as in process in the diagram.

A rather more complicated joining

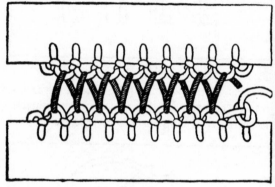

FIG. 76.

stitch is shown in fig. 76. It could be carried out with different coloured threads. The two sides must be first worked with the edging, which is practically the braid stitch described on page 88. Commence the stitch in exactly the same way as when carrying out braid stitch, but work on the edge of the material as

142

in buttonholing, the working edge in this case being away from the worker. Let the worker, having reached the point of pulling the thread through to complete the stitch, draw it out in the direction away from her. This will draw the stitch towards the edge, where it will form a knot. In the diagram one of the stitches has been partly undone in order to show the working more clearly. When the two sides are bound with the stitch, they can be laced together with another thread as in the illustration.

PICOTS

Picots are commonly in use in lace work and they are sometimes required for embroidery purposes, especially in the kinds of work nearly allied to lace, such as cut work, or for an added ornament to an edging stitch.

Fig. 77 shows too small picots added to a buttonhole bar, and on the lower bar is shown the method of working the left-hand picot. The pin that passes into the material behind the bar can be fixed in the bar itself if there happens to

143

be no material underneath. After reaching the point illustrated in the diagram, the needle draws the thread through, thus making a firm knot round the loop.

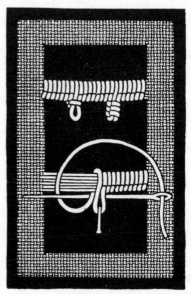

FIG. 77.

This completes the picot, the bar is then buttonholed to the end. The second picot is made in much the same way; instead, however, of putting the needle as the diagram shows, bring the

144

thread up through the centre of the
loop, then round under the pin from left
to right, and it will be in position to
make three buttonhole stitches along

Fig. 78.

the loop, which completes the second
example.

The upper bar on fig. 78 shows a
buttonholed picot. The bar must be
worked to the left-hand end of the

145

required picot; the thread is then from there taken back about one-eighth of an inch and threaded through the edge of the buttonhole. This is repeated to and fro until there is a loop composed of three threads ready to be buttonholed over. Upon this being done, the thread will have arrived at the right point to continue the bar.

Bullion stitch makes another simple picot—Work the bar to the point where the picot is required, then, instead of taking the next stitch, insert the point of the needle in the heading of the last stitch. Leave the needle in this position, and twist the thread six or eight times round the point of it, just as for the bullion knot (fig. 59). Place the left thumb over the tight coil thus formed, and pull the needle and thread through tightly in order to make the stitch double up into a tight semi-circle, then continue the buttonholing to the end of the bar.

CHAPTER VII

CANVAS WORK AND STITCHES

CANVAS work, known in the XIIIth century as *opus pulvinarium* or cushion work, is of great antiquity, and seems to have had an independent origin in several countries. It is sometimes given the misleading name of tapestry, perhaps owing to hangings of all kinds being called tapestries, whether loom-woven, worked with the needle, or painted. Large wall hangings with designs similar to those of woven tapestries have been most successfully carried out on canvas in cross or tent stitch; as a rule, however, smaller objects are worked, such as furniture coverings, screens or cushions, whence it is obvious canvas work received its ancient and descriptive Latin name. Many Eastern carpets are worked upon a

Canvas
Work and
Stitches

147

strong canvas in a kind of tent stitch, and so come under the heading of canvas work. It is a particularly durable method of embroidering, and this makes it suitable for use upon anything subjected to hard wear.

The work has usually a very decided and attractive character of its own. A familiar example of this can be seen in the XVIIIth century samplers. Its peculiar character is perhaps due to the fact that it cannot break away from a certain conventionality due to constant use of the same stitch, and its dependence upon the web of the fabric. This regularity prevents the work from showing certain faults of design that other methods may exaggerate. It is hardly possible to copy a natural spray of flowers in cross stitch and keep it very naturalistic. The stitch being square and alike all over gives a formality of treatment to every part of the design, also, some detail is perforce omitted owing to the impossibility of putting it in; all of this tends to a right method of treatment, which renders the sampler an admirable lesson not only in workmanship but also in design.

148

The XVIth and XVIIth century pictorial subjects worked upon fine canvas in cross or tent stitch afford instances of most interesting work in canvas stitches. Some of these, though, as a rule, very much smaller in size, equal, in their way, the finest tapestries. Most of them, if judged from a painter's standpoint, would be pronounced failures, but this effect is not what is sought after; the method of treatment belongs rather to the great traditions of the tapestry weaver, and is not governed by the canons of the painter. Plate VI. shows a detail of foliage from a particularly fine example of this work lately added to the Victoria and Albert Museum collection.[1]

In what went by the name of Berlin wool work, popular in the early XIXth century, we have before us a degenerate offshoot of this fine and poetic kind of work in which all its possibilities are missed, with a result that is prosaic in the extreme. Some of the canvas-work seat covers decorated with geometrical designs, seen on Chippendale chairs, were a pleasant and satisfactory variation in

[1] No. 879, 1904.

their way, but in most of the work after
that period, the attempt at impossible
naturalistic effect gave such unsatisfactory
results as to almost deal a death blow
to all canvas embroidery. It is, however,
a method too good and useful to die
out; it must always be more or less in
vogue.

Patterns carried out in canvas stitches
are sometimes to be seen worked apparently
upon velvet or similar ground materials.
This is done by first laying the canvas
upon the velvet and stitching through both
materials; this would have to be carried
out in a frame. The threads of the
canvas are afterwards either withdrawn
or closely cut off. In the former case,
the stitches must be drawn tight, or
the finished work will not look well.
This method has the advantage of saving
the labour of working the background,
and sometimes it suits the pattern to
have a contrast in the ground material.
In old embroideries, heraldic devices
may be seen successfully treated in this
way.

The usual canvas stitches can be worked
upon other fabrics that have an even and
square mesh, such as various kinds of

150

linen; also other embroidery stitches, such as stem, satin, or chain, can be used upon canvas; they are then always worked with a certain regularity, following the web of the material.

Canvas work can be done in the hand or in a frame, but the technique is often better in work done in a frame. In all-over work it is important that not even a suggestion of the ground fabric should be allowed to show through; for this reason work in light colours should be done on white canvas, and *vice versâ*, as far as possible, also the thread used must suit in thickness the mesh of the canvas. To work a plain ground well is less easy than to work the pattern, though it may sound more simple. The back of the work, though not necessarily similar to the front, must be alike in stitch all over, for the direction the stitch takes at the back affects the regularity of appearance of the front. The stitch must not be commenced in exactly the same place in each row, lest a ridge should appear upon the surface; this can be avoided by using threads of different lengths. A ground is usually commenced at the lower left - hand corner, and a pattern, if a complicated

151

one, from the centre outwards. These technical points are of importance, but they are of little value unless the stitches are at the same time expressing an interesting and suitable design.

The stitches used are exceedingly numerous; those described in the following pages are the varieties most commonly seen.

Cross stitch, the best known in this group, can be worked in slightly different ways, according to the purpose for which it is required. On the surface it is always the same, but it can vary at the back. For instance, when used for marking purposes it should form on the reverse side either a cross or a square, to do either of which demands some ingenuity on the part of the worker. For ordinary work the really correct method is to complete each stitch before going on to the next, though grounding is frequently done by working the first half of the stitch along an entire line, and completing the cross upon a return journey. In any case, the crossing must always be worked in the same direction.

Cross stitch is a double stitch worked diagonally over two threads of the canvas each way. It can, however, be taken over more or fewer threads if required larger or smaller. To work it (fig. 79)—Bring the needle through on the upper left side of the threads to be covered, and take it back again on the lower right, then bring it through on the upper right

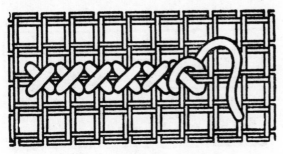

FIG. 79.

side and return it to the back on the lower left, which completes the first stitch.

Tent stitch (fig. 80) is the finest canvas stitch, and is therefore suitable for work involving much detail. Pictorial and heraldic subjects are frequently carried out in it. It is worked diagonally over a perpendicular and horizontal thread of the canvas. The diagram shows the

153

method of working both back and front.
It will be noticed that though the line
goes alternately from left to right and
from right to left, the stitch is always the
same at the back as well as the same
upon the front; if this were not so,
alternate rows would have a different
appearance upon the right side. The

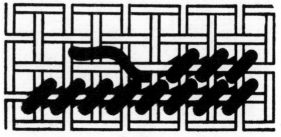

FIG. 80.

diagram does not show the connection
between the first and the second row,
but it is evident that it must be a short
upright line.

Gobelin stitch is a useful variety; it lends
itself to shading better than cross stitch.
It is most often worked upon a fine single
canvas, and it can be used as a raised stitch.
Fig. 81 represents the stitch; it is worked
similarly to tent stitch but over two threads

154

in height and one in width, no matter whether the single or double thread canvas is used. In order to work it as a raised stitch, a line of some kind of padding is thrown across the canvas, and the stitch taken over it. This line can be arranged to show in part, in which case the material must be one presentable,

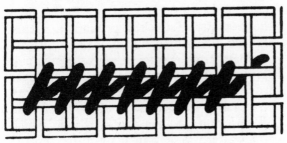

FIG. 81.

such as a gold cord or narrow braid. The padding would be covered with stitching to form the background, and left exposed for the pattern, which would probably be a simple repeating form of some kind. Gobelin stitch is sometimes worked quite perpendicularly just over two threads in height.

Irish stitch is pretty and quickly worked. It is usually taken perpendicularly over

155

four threads of the canvas (fig. 82),
though the number over which it is
taken may vary. It is worked in such
a way as to make the stitches of each
succeeding row fit between those of the
last row, and can be carried out either
diagonally or in horizontal lines. What
is known as Florentine work is carried
out in a stitch of this kind. The
pattern in this kind of work is taken
horizontally across the ground in a succession of shaded zigzag lines.

Plait stitch is often used for grounding.
It resembles a simple plait laid in close
rows to and fro on the ground. It can
frequently be seen used upon the Italian
XVIth century linen work, that in which
the pattern is left in plain linen, and the
ground worked in some colour. The
diagram in fig. 83 shows the method
of working the stitch. If carried out
correctly, the back of the material should
show a row of short perpendicular lines,
each composed of two threads.

Two-sided Italian stitch is descriptively
named, for it is alike on both sides.
This is frequently seen on XVIth and
XVIIth century Italian linen work, similar
to that mentioned above. A loosely

156

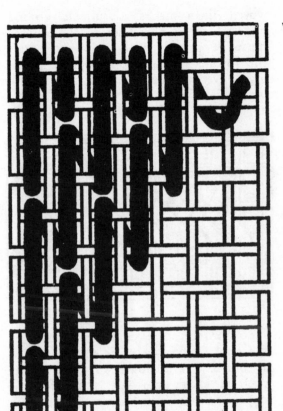

FIG. 82.

woven linen makes a suitable ground
material, for in the working the stitches
must be pulled firmly, so as to draw
the threads of the fabric together; this
gives over the ground a squared open-
work effect, which is very pretty. Fig. 84
explains the working of the stitch; it is

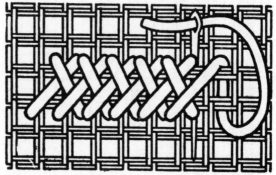

FIG. 83.

shown in four stages, and is quite simple;
the final result is a cross surrounded by
a square. The lowest figure in the
diagram shows the last stage, for the
upper side of the square is filled in
when the row above is worked. The
drawing together of the web is not
shown, but at a trial it should be done,
for in that lies the special character

158

of the stitch. The silk used must be just thick enough to well cover the linen, but not too thick, for then the work would be clumsy.

Holbein stitch (fig. 85), also known as stroke or line stitch, is alike on both sides, and is often used in conjunction with cross and satin stitch, as well as alone. Very intricate and interesting patterns can be devised to be carried out with these three stitches, worked always with regard to the web

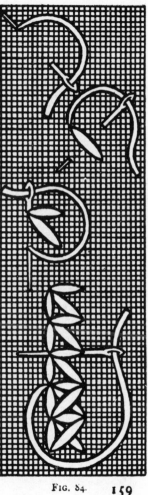

FIG. 84.

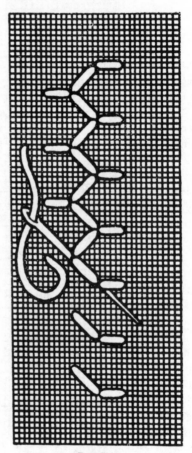

FIG. 85.

of the linen. Squared paper could be used for planning the design, as the stitches would all be practically of the same length, and the pattern must be one that can be easily carried out alike on both sides. The stitch is worked as follows: An even running stitch, picking up as much material as it leaves, is taken all round the pattern. This does half the work on either side; the gaps are then filled up by the running stitch being taken in a contrary direction, which completes the pattern. Occasionally stitches go off at

FIG. 86.

an angle from the running pattern;
these are completed on the first journey
by a satin stitch being made at the
necessary point. The present diagram
is a zigzag line, with one of these stitches
going off at each angle. Fig. 86 is an

FIG. 87.

example of a border design carried out
in Holbein stitch.

The stitch illustrated in fig. 87 is
known as rococo stitch. It is a useful one
for carrying out a conventional design,
such as, to give a simple illustration, a
flower sprig repeating in the spaces formed
by a trellis pattern. The effect of the
stitch when worked cannot be judged

162

from this diagram; to see this properly a piece of canvas must be worked entirely over with it. The pattern chosen is usually one that lends itself to being worked in diagonal lines, as this stitch is best worked in that way. It entirely hides the canvas background, and is carried out very similarly to the oriental stitch in fig. 71. By the help of that diagram and description and the present one, which gives various steps, the worker will easily master the stitch, which is quite simple. The ordinary carrying out of the stitch is shown where the needle is at work, and in another part the diagram, by some loosened stitches, illustrates how to pass from one cluster to the next.

Some fine examples of canvas work design, introducing a variety of stitches. may be seen in the Victoria and Albert Museum. These are large panels filled with foliage and flowers growing about architectural columns.[1]

[1] No. 517-522, 1896.

CHAPTER VIII

METHODS OF WORK

Couching — Braid Work — Laid Work — Applied
Work—Inlaid Work—Patch Work

COUCHING

COUCHING is the name given to a method
of embroidery in which one thread is
attached to the material by another one.
Sometimes not only one thread but a
number of threads are couched down
together; or it may be cord, braid,
or metal thread that is attached to the
material in this way. Fig. 88 shows
some couching in progress. The method
probably arose through the difficulty experienced in passing either coarse or very
delicate threads through a material.
Couching is constantly in use with gold
thread embroidery, and it is further discussed in the chapter upon that subject,
where also is described an entirely different
method, which is to be recommended
for couching other as well as for gold
threads.

164

Couching is useful in a variety of ways, *e.g.* for carrying out work in line or for outlining other embroidery, applied work for instance, which is frequently finished off by means of a couched

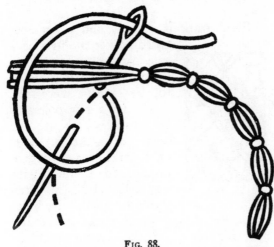

FIG. 88.

thread; in the case of a difficult ground material, it is one of the most manageable methods of working. The geometrical open fillings of leaves and backgrounds are often composed of lines of thread thrown across and couched down at regular intervals. Fig. 89 is an example

165

of a favourite filling of this kind. Embroidery stitches can be made use of for couching down other threads; a bunch of threads may be laid upon the material, and an open chain, buttonhole, or feather stitch worked over in order to fix it in place.

Braid work is quickly and easily executed; it needs only a suitable pattern and a pretty braid for couching down to be most successful. There are a few points to be observed about the technique — the cut edge of a braid is awkward to manage, for it must, with a special needle, be taken through to the back of the material and there made secure and flat; for this reason the design should be so planned as to have as few breaks as possible. Interlacing strap work designs, of which a simple example is given in fig. 90, are very suitable for braid work. The thread that couches down the braid may be quite invisible, or, on the other hand, it may be made use of to further decorate the braid by being placed visibly across it,

FIG. 89.

perhaps forming a chequering or other simple pattern, as shown in fig. 91. Ravellings of the braid may be used as invisible couching threads for stitching

FIG. 90.

it down. Curves and sharp corners need special attention by way of extra stitches. The completed work is much improved by several hours' pressure under a weight.

167

Laid work might be described as couching on a more extended scale—a given space is covered with threads taken from side to side in parallel lines close together, fixed at either extremity by entering the material. Further security is usually given by small couching stitches dotted down at intervals over the laid threads,

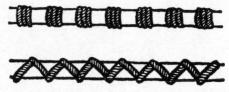

FIG. 91.

or by throwing single lines of thread across in a contrary direction and tying these down at intervals with couching stitches. Yet another way is, to work a split or stem stitch over the laid threads, and thus fix them down. Fig. 92 shows a flower carried out in laid work. The tying-down threads can often be made use of in one way or another to further decorate, or to explain form, by means of contrasting colour, change in direction,

168

and so on. The laid stitches in this flower
are taken from the centre outwards and
fixed in place by couched circular lines of

FIG. 92.

thread. The centre of the flower has a
geometrical filling, composed of a couched
lattice pattern with French knots between.

169

Conventional centres of this and like kinds
are very pretty for embroidery flowers;
such patterns as those shown in fig. 93
can often be seen in
use, and they need only
a trial to be frequently
adopted.

FIG. 93.

Laid work shows off
the gloss and texture of
silk to great advantage,
which is due to the
thread being laid upon
the material without
being cut up into small
stitches. Floss silk is
much used for the
work; it must not be
at all twisted in the
laying down, since this
mars the effect. The
work is carried out in a frame; it is quickly
executed and economical, the thread being
practically all upon the surface. Owing
to the length of the stitches, this is not
a very durable method, so it should not be
subjected to hard wear. The work has
sometimes a flimsy, unsatisfactory appearance, probably because of these long stitches.
It will be seen that the silk passing through

to the back, and then immediately to the
front again, takes up very little of the

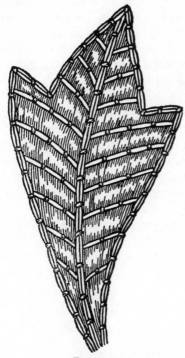

FIG. 94.

material. A method in use for giving
greater strength in this way is to lay the
silk first in alternate lines and to fill up

171

the gaps thus left upon a second journey
across the form. For added strength, use
might be made of a linen thread at the
back, as in the *point couché rentré ou retiré*
method that is discussed later.

A gold thread outline gives a nice finish
to laid work. If there is nothing in the
way of an outline, and the pattern and
ground are both covered with laid threads,
the edges of the pattern are likely to
look weak. Fig. 94 shows a leaf filled
in with rather loosely laid threads and
outlined and veined with gold passing,
the veining answering the double purpose
of fixing down the laid threads and veining the leaf at the same time.

In this work, the colouring is frequently in flat tones, but if necessary it is
quite easy to introduce gradation. Further
variety can be obtained by a contrast in
colour in the tying-down threads.

APPLIED WORK

The ancient Latin term *opus consutum*,
and the modern French one *appliqué*, which
is perhaps the name most commonly in
use, both refer to the same kind of work;
what is now called cut work is quite

172

different from this, and is described elsewhere. Under the heading of applied
work comes anything that, cut out of
one material, is applied to another;
it may have been previously embroidered,
or it may be just the plain stuff. Both
kinds can, as has been proved, be carried
out with excellent effect, but much unsuitable and badly designed work has been
done by this method, with the result that
the very name has fallen into disrepute.

The simplest kind of applied work is
that in which the design, traced upon
one material, then cut out along the outline of the pattern, is applied to another
material, the junction of the two materials being hidden by a cord or suitable
stitch. The applied work is most often
flat, but it can be in slight or in strong
relief. The texture of the materials employed may be an important factor in the
result, for a contrast in material as well
as in colour is often wanted; sometimes
the former alone is sufficient. The choice
of material depends very much upon the
use to which the finished work will be
put, but this simple form of applied work
often relies for part of its effect upon an
intrinsic interest in the material, so it is

173

usually carried out with such materials as velvet, satin, or silk, either plain or figured.

The design for this kind of work should be of a bold conventional type, such as large foliage with the character of the heraldic mantling; any naturalistic flowers, figures, or animals easily become grotesque. A simple outline to the forms is necessary, both because of the technical difficulties and for the effect of the finished work. This kind of work is hardly suitable for expressing fine detail; oftentimes it is seen from a distance, and many indentations on an outline sometimes tend to weaken it. Heraldry can be well expressed by this method. Fig. 95 is an example from a piece of XIIIth century work, a fragment of the surcoat of William de Fortibus, third Earl of Albemarle, who lived in the reign of Henry III.; the example can be seen in the British Museum. This method of work is also particularly suitable for such purposes as the decoration of wall surfaces, for hangings of various kinds, or banners; it can, however, be used for many other purposes, provided the design and the materials are well chosen.

Owing to the difficulty of working upon some ground stuffs, the method has arisen of carrying out the embroidery upon an easily worked ground, such as linen; cutting it out, when finished, along

FIG. 95.

the outline and applying it to the proper ground, the junction of the two materials being hidden by a cord or some equivalent. It is usually further completed by

175

light sprays or some other kind of finishing touches being placed around the
applied part, these worked directly on
to the proper ground. This prevents the
embroidery from looking too bald and
detached from its surroundings, of which
there is always a danger when it is carried
out separately and then attached; if at
all possible it is always more satisfactory
to work directly on to the right ground.

As a matter of fact it is almost always
possible to do this; the workers of the
XIIIth century, the period at which the
art of embroidery was at its height,
carried out the most exquisitely fine
stitching and design on such grounds as
velvet that had almost as long a pile as
some varieties of plush. The famous
cope of English work known as the
Bowden cope, of which a detail is given
in Plate I., is an excellent illustration of
this point. Upon careful examination of
the work it is apparent that between
the stitching and the velvet there is a
layer of material, composed either of
fine linen or silk. This would be of great
help in the carrying out of the stitching.
It is exceedingly probable that this layer
of fine material was at the commencement

of the work laid completely over the velvet background of the cope; for one thing, the design, with its finely drawn detail, could easily be perfectly traced upon a surface of this kind and only imperfectly upon velvet; another advantage of this method would be, that the background would be kept quite free from dust and from getting soiled by the hands during the lengthy process of the work. The stitching would be carried through all the surfaces, and when finished, the fine surface layer would be cut away close round the edges of the design, which would be quite easily done. This method of working upon a difficult ground is well worth trying in place of the applied method.

To return to the discussion of applied embroidery—let us suppose the embroidered piece to be just completed on its linen ground, still stretched in the frame in which it was worked. In another frame, stretch the background material and trace upon it the exact outline of the piece to be applied. Cut out the embroidered piece carefully round the edge, allowing about one-sixteenth of an inch margin outside the worked part, leaving, if necessary, little connect-

ing ties of material here and there for
temporary support. With fine steel pins
or needles fix the cut-out work exactly
over the tracing already made on the
ground material, then make it secure
round the edge with rather close stitches
of silk placed at right-angles to the outline; with fine materials the raw edge
of the applied part can be neatly tucked
under and fixed in place by this overcast
stitch. A cord is next sewn on to hide
the fixing and give a finish to the edge.
The colour of this cord is important,
since its colour may increase the expanse
of either the applied part or the ground.
Sometimes a double cord is put round,
and in this case the inner one is attached
to the embroidery before it is cut out of
the frame, and the second attached afterwards. The inner one is often of a colour
predominating in the embroidery, and
the outer one of the colour of the ground.
Gold cord is very usual; if a coloured silk
one is used it must be a perfect match.
The ordinary twisted cord looks best
attached invisibly; to do this, slightly un-
twist it whilst stitching and insert the
needle in the opening thus formed. Some
kinds of flat braids look well with the

178

fixing stitches taken deliberately over them
and forming part of the ornamentation
(see fig. 91). Bunches of silk are sometimes couched round with a buttonhole or
other stitch, but whatever the outline may
consist of, it should be a firm bold line.

The work must be perfectly flat when
completed. Puckering may occur through
want of care in the preliminary straining
or in the fixing on of the applied parts.
Some materials are more easy to manage
than others. The difficult ones can if
necessary have a preliminary backing
applied, which is useful also if the
material is inclined to fray. The backing may consist of a thin coating of
embroidery paste, or of tissue paper or
fine holland pasted over the part to be
applied. The more all this kind of thing
can be avoided, the better the work, for
pasting of any kind is apt to give a stiff
mechanical look; also, if the work is
intended to hang in folds any stiffness
would be most impracticable.

Even more than simpler work applied
embroidery needs the finish of some
light work upon the ground. Gold
threads and spangles, arranged in fashion
similar to the sprays in fig. 112, are

179

very often used. Sometimes, instead of this, some small pattern in outline is run all over the ground in order to enrich it.

INLAID WORK

Inlaid work is in effect similar to the applied, and it is used for the same purposes. The difference with this is that both background and pattern are cut out and fitted into each other, instead of only one of them being cut out and laid on an entire ground. The method of work is economical, for there need be very little waste of material. What is left from cutting out the pattern and background for one piece can be used as ground and pattern for another and possibly companion piece. There is in Perugia a church which possesses a complete set of draperies of this description, that were made at a good period for this work, early XVIth century, and evidently were designed for the position they occupy. On festivals, the piers, pulpit, and parts of the wall are hung with these rose and gold-coloured hangings of inlaid work. The design is a conventional scroll-work pattern, and the various hangings have alternately the rose ground with gold pattern, and gold ground with rose pattern, the whole forming a rich and harmonious interchange of colour.

Fig. 96 is an example of inlaid work.

FIG. 96.

It is a XVth century tabard said to have belonged to Charles the Bold, and now in the Musée Historique at Berne. The pattern, it will be noticed, is planned on the counterchange principle, which is particularly well suited for this method of work.

A very ancient piece of the same kind of inlaid work is the funeral tent of Queen Isi-em-Keb, dated about 980 B.C., which is in the Boulak Museum, Cairo. It is composed of thousands of pieces of gazelle hide dyed in various colours and stitched together so as to form a wonderful design.[1]

To carry out the work—Stitch in a frame some holland to use as a background; this may be only temporary, being removed when the work is completed, or it may be left for additional strength. The materials for both background and pattern must first be carefully cut out. It is a good plan, where possible, to cut the two together so as to ensure exact similarity, for they have to fit together afterwards like the parts of a puzzle. The cut edges cannot be allowed to fray, so if there is any danger of this, precautions must be taken to prevent it, though the better way is to choose in the first place more suitable material. Leather is a particularly good example of one. Any pasting or backing which might be used for prevention of

[1] For further information see "The Funeral Tent of an Egyptian Queen," by Villiers Stuart.

fraying would prevent also that possibility of exposing both sides of the work, which in inlay is sometimes a valuable quality; also, the stiffening which unavoidably results from pasting is rarely an improvement. When materials of different thicknesses are used together, the thinner one can be lined with fine holland so as to make it nearer equal in strength. After the materials are cut out the next process is to lay them in position on the prepared holland and tack them to it. Then, with an overcast stitch that must not be allowed to pierce the under surface, join all the edges together, and cover the stitches with a finishing cord or braid. The backing can now be removed if need be.

PATCHWORK

Patchwork can hardly attain to a high position amongst the various branches of embroidery. The main object of doing patchwork frequently is to make good use of valuable scraps of waste material. Unless, however, the product shows evidence of well thought out colour and arrangement, it cannot come under the heading

183

of embroidery. Interesting results, however, of many kinds can be produced from
this paint-box of brightly coloured scraps
of material by ingenious mixing and shap-
ing of them. Patchwork infers a rather
more mosaic-like design than inlaid work,
to which it is in some respects similar.
The geometrically planned mosaic and
inlay pavements that are to be seen so
commonly in Italy and the East suggest
great variety of patterns that could be
applied to patchwork. The illustration
at fig. 97 is a simple example taken
from this source. Too often the results
are only "alarming," as the Countess
of Wilton expressively puts it, thinking,
probably, of the patterns frequently seen
upon cushions, patterns more resembling
bright-coloured bricks set in cornerwise
than anything else. They are the most
unrestful looking things imaginable. The
important elements of the work lie in
the colour, shape, and texture of the
pieces used, for upon the right selection
the result wholly depends. The shapes
chosen must be simple owing to the
necessity of fitting and stitching them
together, but there is plenty of variety
obtainable with simplicity. The design

184

may consist of one shape repeated or several. If only one, it is limited to a

FIG. 97.

few geometrical figures, such as the square, hexagon, or shell shape; if more

185

than one, there can be greater variety
of pattern. Fig. 98 is an example in
which four shapes are made use of, a
large and small circle, an octagon, and
an S-like twist. Four of these twists
together make the figure that interlaces
over the surface. Embroidery stitching
can be added to patchwork; for instance,
this example might have a neat border
pattern worked on all the S-shapes, as
suggested in the diagram, which would
probably considerably increase its interest.
Fig. 99 shows flowers springing from the
base of the shell-form in use upon it.
The embroidery could be simply carried
out in one colour, or if a more gorgeous
result were required, variety could be
introduced in this way as well as in the
ground, and a marvellous combination of
intricate colour could be thus produced.

For the work to be made up satisfactorily it is necessary that the shapes be
accurately cut out. To ensure this, a
metal plate is cut and all the shapes are
taken from it; sometimes, in lieu of this,
a pattern is cut out in stiff cardboard.
Lay this pattern-shape on the wrong
side of the material and pencil it round,
then carefully cut out the stuff, leaving

186

FIG. 98.

187

about a quarter of an inch for turning in. Next lay the pattern-shape upon a piece of stiff paper or thin card-board and again trace off the shape, this time cutting it out exactly to the pattern, tack the material to the paper, and stitch

FIG. 99.

down the raw edges at the back. Lay the prepared patches on a table and put them in place by referring to the design, and then commence sewing the edges together with an overcast stitch on the wrong side. When all are sewn, remove the papers and flatten the seams with

188

an iron. Any braid or stitch that may be required to mask the join is next put on ; this may be made ornamental by interlacing knots at the corners, or by any other device that happens to suit the work. The last thing to be done is to put a neat lining upon the back to cover and protect the numerous raw edges.

CHAPTER IX

METHODS OF WORK——(*continued*)

Quilting—Raised Work—Darning—Open Fillings—
Darned Netting.

QUILTING is a method of working by which three materials are fixed together by more or less all-over stitching. It probably developed through the necessity of keeping the three layers in place. For practical purposes only, the sewing machine does the work excellently, but by making the stitching follow out some prearranged design, it is raised to the level of art. Plate III. is an interesting example showing what can be done in the way of design with the stitching over the surface. Embroidery may be added to the quilting.

189

and this is often an improvement. The
Eastern nations carry out marvellously
intricate designs in quilting, and English
XVIIIth century work of this kind shows
Eastern influence strongly. A good
example of this is a very interesting
piece in the Victoria and Albert
Museum.[1]

The first aim in quilting was evidently
warmth, and the name denotes one of the
chief uses to which it is put. It is made
use of also for curtains, infants' caps
or gloves (see fig. 100), all these
things requiring the three layers for
warmth. The materials usually consist
of a surface one, which can be silk, fine
linen or anything else; an interlining of
some softer material having a certain
amount of spring in it, such as flannel,
cotton wadding, or wool; and for the
third, an underneath lining of some kind.
A cord is sometimes inserted instead of
the inner layer of stuff, the lines of stitching running along either side to keep it in
place. Occasionally there are only the top
and the under layer, with no intervening
material. The stitch usually employed
is a running, back, or chain stitch, and

[1] No. 1564, 1902.

Fig. 100.

191

it can be of the colour of the surface, or
a contrast to it. Gold silk is often seen
upon a white linen ground. The chief
interest in the work lies in the choice of
pattern, such things as colour, variety of
stitching, interest in material, are not
made much of. In planning the pattern,
use is made of the knowledge that the
closely stitched parts will lie more flatly,
so it frequently happens that the ground
has a small diaper running over it, and
the pattern part, being less worked upon,
perhaps only outlined, stands out more
and forms an effective contrast.

RAISED WORK

In the XIVth century raised work
was commonly done, but few examples
are known of date earlier than this.
The raised effect is obtained by an interposed layer of padding, which is a good
method of getting a certain kind of
effect. It is perhaps wise to err on the
side of too little rather than too much
relief. An example of too much and also
of a wrong kind is the English stump
work that was popular in the XVIIth
century, when figures were stuffed like

dolls, the clothes made separately and attached, even to the shoes and stockings. Germain de St. Aubin, writing in 1769, describes with much admiration a kind of *broderie en ronde bosse*, apparently much the same thing and in equally doubtful taste, though the skill required to carry it out must have been considerable.

The work, usually done in a frame, must be well carried out technically; the padding should be quite perfect in the form required before the final surface layer is worked over it, for this one will not make any deficiency right, but will only serve to show it up the more. Another point to be careful about is to make the padding stop well within the traced line of the pattern, otherwise the finished design will turn out much larger than was originally intended. The outline is sometimes worked round at the commencement, whereby its correctness is ensured.

Many different materials are brought into use for padding purposes. One of the simplest and most durable is a running of thread as illustrated in fig. 101. The thread can be arranged so

as to be thicker in the centre than at
the edges by laying some extra stitches
over that part. If a quite flat padding

,s required, the shape, cut out in cloth,
felt, or parchment, is attached by stitches
to the material as shown in fig. 102;
the surface stitching would
be taken across it. Card-
board, sometimes pasted on
to the ground, is used for
this purpose, but it is unsatisfactory in several ways;
for instance, cardboard letters are procurable for embroidering initials upon
linen, but they are not at
all practical for anything
that goes through the wash;
moreover, the letters are

FIG. 102.

sometimes of bad design. Cotton wool is
used as a stuffing, its surface being usually
covered over with muslin, but this again

194

would not stand much wear of any kind, and so could only be used under certain conditions.

Another good method is to couch down a hank of threads of fine cotton or perhaps wool as illustrated in fig.

FIG. 103.

103. For raised lines there is a special kind of string procurable that can be couched to the ground material at the required places. The padding, whatever it may be composed of, should be as nearly as possible of the same colour as the surface layer, in view of any after wear and tear misplacing the threads.

The top layer of underlay must lie in direction contrary to

FIG. 104.

the surface embroidery stitching, which is very often some form of satin stitch taken from side to side over the padding. Instead of going through the material it can

195

be fixed on each side with a couching
stitch, as in fig. 104. A stronger way
than these would be that shown in fig.
129. Buttonhole is a good stitch for
working over a padding; it would be
worked solidly in the manner described
and illustrated on page 117, but taken,
as there shown, over a padding instead
of over a flat surface.

DARNING

There is a most practical sound about
darning; it can, however, be made good
use of in embroidery as well as in plain
needlework. There are two rather different kinds in use; in both the stitch is
a running one and done in much the
same way that a thin place would be
darned in mending.

One kind of darning is rather popular
at the present moment, and examples of it
may be familiar; it is a large, bold kind
of work, often carried out with a coarse
twisted silk. Upon the background, the
lines of stitching usually run straight
across or up and down, in the pattern,
they radiate according to the shape of the
form to be filled. The entire material

is covered one way or another by the running stitches, and just one thread of the ground fabric is picked up where necessary at irregular intervals; a loosely woven linen is often chosen for working upon, one in which it is easy to pick up the single thread. Gradation of colour can easily be introduced; the design chosen is most frequently some kind of conventional flower and leafy scroll. This method of embroidery is seen to best advantage when used upon large surfaces.

The second kind is called pattern darning; in it the stitches are picked up in some regular order, so that they form various geometrical patterns over the surface. It is worked by counting the threads of the fine linen ground and picking up a single thread or more in some regular sequence. The threads are run in parallel lines close together, either horizontally or vertically, so as to take advantage of the web of the fabric. The work is particularly pretty and not difficult, requiring only patience and good eyesight. Fig. 105 gives some simple examples of the work—The first is a chevron pattern, formed by picking up one thread and leaving about five each

197

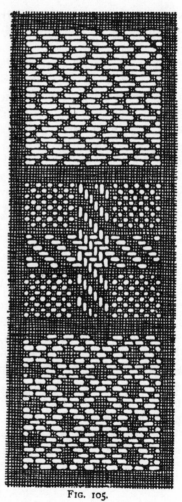

FIG. 105.

time; each succeeding row moves a step
forward or backward as required to carry
out the pattern. In the second example
the darning is taken two ways of the
material; in the centre, where it meets
and crosses, it entirely covers the ground.
A different colour might be used for each
direction, which would look very well at
the crossing in the centre. The four
corners are filled up with a chequer darn;
this each time picks up as much material
as it leaves. The third example shows
the darning stitch forming a diamond
pattern. Samplers, dated early XIXth
century, may be seen entirely filled with
these pattern darns; they are covered
with most intricate and beautiful sample
squares showing various patterns in darning, and were possibly done in order to
learn how to repair damask table linen.
In a collection of early Egyptian work
in the Victoria and Albert Museum, there
is some pattern darning, dated VIth to
IXth century, A.D., which proves it to be
a very early method of embroidering.

This pattern darning, however, is so
pretty that it is often possible to make use
of it in embroidery work for all kinds of
purposes. It makes a very good back-

ground if there is sufficient space to
show the pattern,
if there is not, the
irregular darning
might be used in-
stead, for it would
in that case be just
as good and much
quicker to work.
To pattern-darn
the ground with
the ornament upon
it left in the plain
material, perhaps
not worked upon
at all, is a very
effective method
of carrying out a
design, see fig. 106
for example. Again
it might very well
be used for the con-
ventional carrying
out of draperies in
the same way as in
*point couché rentré
ou retiré.*[1] The
draperies on the

FIG. 106.

[1] For description of this method, see page 238.

200

figure in the frontispiece could easily be
carried out with silk thread in the darning stitch, in fact this method of decoration more closely resembles the early
couching than any other; it is not quite
as satisfactory because the single threads
of the background that are picked up
prevent the ground showing nothing but
silk. Bands of this work may be seen
ornamenting needle books or work cases;
it shows to best advantage when worked
finely with floss or filosel silk, the coarse
twisted silks are too thick for the purpose.

OPEN WORK FILLINGS

Patterns can be carried out in line,
they can be worked quite solidly, and
there is a method that lies between these
two known as open filling. The open
and solid fillings are often used together
in the same piece of work; examples
of this can be seen on the XVIIth
century wool-work curtains, the large
scrolling leaves are sometimes partly
worked openly and a portion, possibly
reflexed, filled in with solid stitches in
gradating colour; see for an example Plate
VIII. This has a very good effect, it

201

prevents the work looking too heavy, shows up the form more clearly, and allows of more variety in the stitching. With open fillings the outline surrounding them must always be some firm decided line, such as is made by a band of satin or long and short stitch, or, in the case of larger forms, by several rows of different line stitches worked closely together, one inside the other, most likely in different shades of colour. A filling of open work can be carried out in a variety of ways; it

FIG. 107.

may be a decorated trellis, a regular dotting of some kind, or some geometrical pattern in outline, or some light stitch such as an open buttonhole (see fig. 107), which would be treated each as a diapering over the form to be filled. It does not much matter what the filling

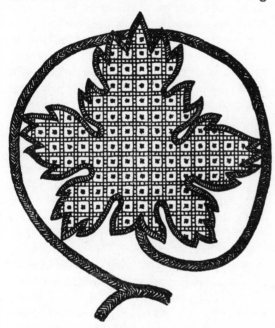

FIG. 108.

is as long as it is dispersed pretty regularly over the space, giving the effect at a little distance of a light pervading tone, and when examined closely exhibiting an in-

203

teresting small pattern. The open filling
method can be used entirely throughout
a design with very pretty effect; an example of this may be seen on an embroidered coverlet and pillow case in
the Victoria and Albert Museum.[1] The
pattern, composed of vine leaves and
grapes, is carried out in dark brown silk
on a linen ground, the leaves being all
outlined with satin stitch. There is wonderful variety in the patterns, no two
alike, which form the open fillings of the
leaves; this makes them most interesting
to examine, and is evidence of enthusiasm
in their designing. Fig. 108, a leaf taken
from this specimen, shows one method of
filling a form with open work.[2] Fig. 109
shows a collection of patterns taken
from the same piece of embroidery.
It will be observed that small stitches
of the same length compose the pattern,
which can be designed upon squared
paper and easily copied on to the linen
ground by always picking up the same
number of threads. To look well these
little forms must be accurately worked.

[1] A piece belonging to Lord Falkland.
[2] Fig. 18 is a drawing from the border of the same
example.

FIG. 109.

and they or similar kinds can be used
upon flowers, leaves, beasts, draperies,
or anything else quite indiscriminately.
Fig. 110, from a cap in the Victoria and

FIG. 110.

Albert Museum, is a drawing showing
the same kind of open filling in use upon
a bird.[1]

A quicker way of carrying out these
geometrical fillings is by using such forms

[1] No. 308, 1902.

Fig. 111.

207

as a lattice and throwing the lines from
side to side across the shape to be filled,
fixing them down, where they cross each
other, with couching stitches; the interstices left between the threads can be filled
in with little stars, crosses, or dots (see
fig. 111). Buttonhole stitch, if made use
of as an open filling, would be taken
in lines straight across a form, the stitches
being worked possibly two or three closely
together and then a space, and so on.

Fig. 112 suggests another method of
lightly filling a leaf with a conventional
veining and dotting. There is no limit to
the variety which can be obtained in this
method of working.

Open fillings are effective for use upon
any work that is intended to be seen with
a light at the back; they make very decorative the various forms they fill, in such
things as muslin window blinds, curtains,
fire screens, whether hand screens or the
larger type. For articles of this kind
the patterns should be rather more solid
and less lined in character; fig. 113, taken
from a window blind exhibited in the
Victoria and Albert Museum, exemplifies
what is meant; most of the patterns illustrated in fig. 100 could be treated in a

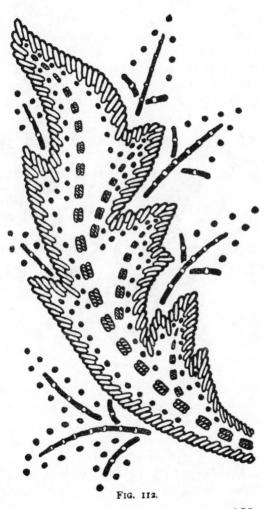

FIG. 112.

more solid manner if necessary, and would
look equally well that way. When working upon transparent grounds special care
must be taken with the reverse side as well
as with the surface, for the work to be practi-

FIG. 113.

cally alike upon both sides; there must be
no threads running from one form to another nor any visible fastening off of ends.

DARNED NETTING

Darned netting, or *lacis*, as it is sometimes called, might almost come under

the heading of either lace or embroidery.
It is used effectively with other kinds of
white linen work, bands or squares of it

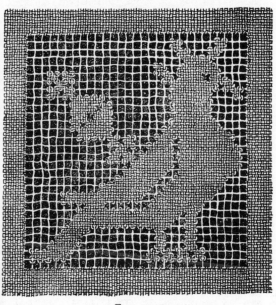

FIG. 114.

being let into the linen; the contrast
of the solid with the more open work
gives a pretty effect. Fig. 114 is an example of this work. The darning is done
on a plain netted ground which can be

211

prepared by the worker if acquainted
with netting, if not, the squares can be
obtained ready for working upon. The
pattern must be designed upon squared
paper as for cross stitch work, then it
is simply a question of following out
the pattern upon the square net ground.
Every square of the patterned part must
be crossed in each direction by two lines
of darning, which should about fill it up.
The various lines are run in and out as
continuously as possible, so as to avoid
unnecessary fastening off or passing from
one part to another. When a fresh thread
is required, join it with a knot to the end
of the last one (see figs. 165 and 166),
and darn the ends in neatly with the
other threads. These knots are often
used in embroidery, for they are both
strong and small. Detached stitches and
parts must be worked by themselves ;
the thread should not be carried from
one to the other. The work must be
done in a frame and carried out with a
blunt-pointed needle. The same thread
is used for the netted ground and for the
darned pattern. A method of work that
the French call *dessein réservé* is, in result,
rather similar to this, but it is worked

212

in just the reverse way. The pattern, whatever it may be, is left in the plain linen, and the background has certain threads in each direction withdrawn at regular intervals, whereby the effect of the squared net ground is obtained.

CHAPTER X

METHODS OF WORK—(*continued*)

Drawn Thread Work—Hem Stitching—Simple Border Patterns—Darned Thread Patterns—Corners—Cut or Open Work—Various Methods of Refilling the Open Spaces.

THIS method of work is the acknowledged link between embroidery and lace, and was possibly the origin of the latter. Drawn work is that in which the threads of either the warp or the weft of the material are withdrawn and those remaining worked into a pattern, by either clustering together or working over them in some fashion. The cut or open work, as it is sometimes called, is that in which both warp and weft are in places cut away, and the open spaces thus formed are partly

213

refilled with a device of one kind or another.

The work is most often carried out in white thread on white linen, but coloured threads may occasionally be introduced with advantage. It is a durable method of work, and particularly suitable for the decoration of various house-linens, things that must undergo daily wear and wash; its rather unobtrusive character too makes it the more suitable for this purpose. The work is used in conjunction with other kinds of embroidery, perhaps making a neat finish to an edge, or lightening what would otherwise be too heavy in appearance.

Drawn thread and cut work can be carried out with such detail and fineness as to really become most delicate lace. In this chapter, however, it is intended to be treated rather as an adjunct to other embroidery, therefore only elementary work will be discussed. More attention might with advantage be paid to the design of this kind of work, for more might be done with it than sometimes is. For one thing, there is very little variety in the patterns, and the result often seems a spidery mass of

incomprehensible threads with no very
perceivable plan; perhaps if more attention were paid to the proportion and
massing of the solid and open parts, a
better result might be attained. Neatness and simplicity are good qualities
in the pattern, the method of work not
being suited to the expression of the
various larger and bolder types of design.

DRAWN THREAD WORK

In drawn work the question is how to
treat the remaining warp threads after the
weft has been withdrawn. They can be
clustered in bunches in different ways with
ornamental stitches added, or be entirely
covered over with darning or overcast
stitches in such a way as to form a
pattern.

The beginning of most drawn thread
work is hem stitching, the two edges
marking the limit of the withdrawn
threads have usually to be hem stitched
before any pattern can be carried out.
One method of doing this is in progress
in fig. 115. In order to work it, draw
out three or four threads of the warp
and tack the hem down to the top edge

215

of the line thus made. The diagram explains the remainder of the working.

Fig. 116 shows in the first example clusters of four threads drawn together at each edge by hem stitching in such a way as to form a ladder-like pattern. This and the one below are the ornamenta-

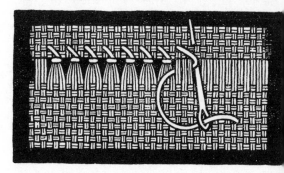

FIG. 115.

tions of a plain hem that are most commonly seen. The variation in pattern in the lower one is obtained by drawing together on the lower edge two threads from two consecutive bunches in the :pper row instead of just repeating over again the same divisioning as before. These two examples are drawn to show the reverse, not the working side.

216

Another way of disposing of the un-drawn threads is to cover them with a kind of darning stitch, as illustrated in fig. 117. This kind of work is more solid than the other, and is for that reason very durable.

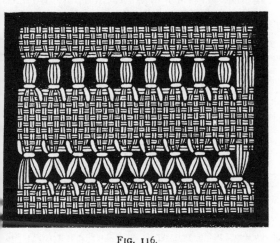

FIG. 116.

This example is commenced at the right-hand corner, where the threads are drawn loosely in order to explain the working. The needle, which should have a blunt point, takes the thread to and fro alter-nately over and under two clusters of warp thread, drawing them together a

217

little during the process; half-way down,
the needle leaves the first set of threads
and continues working with the second
and a new set (see needle in diagram).
When this is worked down to the base the
needle takes the thread invisibly up the
centre of the worked part to the point

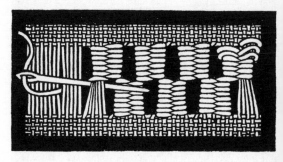

FIG. 117.

where it is required for the continuation
of the pattern. The working of this
simple pattern explains the principle upon
which all kinds of pretty and more complicated designs can be carried out. The
darning thread may be coloured; in a
more intricate design two or three different
colours might be introduced.

Fig. 118 shows another pattern in the
218

same kind of work. The darning stitch
begins by working to and fro over and
under four clusters of warp threads, part
way down it continues over the two central ones only, leaving the outside clusters
alone for the present. It finishes up, as
at the beginning, to and fro over the four.

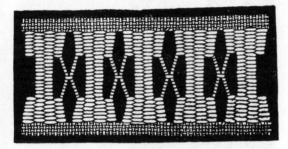

FIG. 118.

The threads that were left are next covered
with an overcast stitch, the adjoining ones
in each case are caught together in the
centre in order to form the X shape that
recurs along the pattern. This darning
kind of work is very closely allied to
weaving, and especially the kind often
seen in Coptic work, in which bands of
the woof threads are purposely omitted
in places, whilst the fabric is being made,

219

in order that a pattern may be hand-woven in afterwards to take their place. Many beautiful examples of this work are on view in the Victoria and Albert Museum.

In working a drawn thread border round a square shape, at each corner there comes an open space that requires a filling. Fig. 119 shows two wheels that are commonly used to ornament such places. The square in the first one has a preliminary groundwork of threads thrown across from corner to corner and from side to side, all meeting and crossing in the centre. The working thread is brought through at this point and the wheel commenced by taking a kind of back stitch over a bar and bringing

FIG. 119.

220

the needle up beyond the next bar. It then takes the thread a step back and over the same bar and brings it up beyond the next; this goes on until the circle is of sufficient size, the stitches growing a little longer in each succeeding row. In the diagram the thread is loosened at the end to explain the working. The lower example is a commonly used wheel, which is made by the thread running round alternately over and under a bar until the wheel is completed. It should be as solid as the upper one, but is purposely left loose in the diagram. Either of the wheels could have a line of buttonhole stitching worked round the edge as a finish. This figure shows also the two usual ways of making firm the raw edges in cut work—the square shape is bound by an overcast stitch, and the round one by buttonholing.

CUT OR OPEN WORK

Cut work can be most interesting both to look at and to carry out. In the XVIIth century Italy was famous for its *punto tagliato* or cut work. John Taylor mentions "rare Italian cutworke" in "The

221

Praise of the Needle." This poem may perhaps be of interest to some; it was prefixed to a book of embroidery patterns of cut work named "The Needle's Excellency." It ran through twelve editions, the first of which was printed in 1621, and sold at "the signe of the Marigold in Paules Churchyard." Copies may be seen in the British Museum Library; in the Bodleian, Oxford, in the Ryland's Library, Manchester, and occasionally elsewhere. Fig. 120 shows a pattern taken from this book.

There are several distinct varieties of cut work, for instance, that known as renaissance embroidery, which is usually composed of an arabesque design from which the background is cut away, leaving the pattern in the linen; the cut edges are outlined and protected by an overcast stitch. The pattern has to be specially planned with the idea of holding strongly together, but, if necessary, buttonholed bars can be added to form strengthening ties in any weak part.

Another kind of cut work is that known as *broderie anglaise*, and sometimes as Madeira work, over which our grandmothers spent much time, perhaps with-

out adequate result. The pattern is
followed out by round holes pierced in
the linen with a stiletto and then overcast
round the edges. At the present day the

FIG. 120.

work is done mostly by machinery, though
hand work also is procurable.

Perhaps the prettiest kind of cut work
is that in which various-shaped spaces are
cut out of the linen, and these filled in, in

223

part, with some design built up with
stitches. There are various methods of
refilling the spaces cut out, one of the
simplest is a diapering formed by some
lace stitch, such as an open buttonhole.
As a rule, the decoration of the open
spaces is based upon bars of thread that
are either composed of warp or woof
threads left, instead of being cut away, or
else upon fresh threads thrown across in
various directions. The pattern is planned
on and about these strengthening ties, and
where necessary receiving support from
them. An ingenious worker will soon
devise ways of refilling the spaces by all
kinds of interesting patterns, which can
be geometrical or floral, or any kinds of
objects that can be attractively represented in conventional fashion, such as
figures, birds, insects, ships in full sail,
or anything else. It must, however, be
remembered that the various forms filling
the spaces are for use in the way of
strength as well as for ornament, and that
the work is often put upon objects that
have to endure daily wear.

Open work is frequently mixed with
other, and especially with white embroidery,
and such things as counterpanes may be

seen arranged with a chequering of alternate squares of embroidered linen and open work.

Fig. 121 shows in progress a simple method of filling a space, mainly making use of the strengthening threads that have been left at regular intervals over the cut part. The threads are covered with an overcast stitch, and alternate squares of those that recur over the space are decorated with a cross. This is made by the working thread, after reaching the right point at the centre of an overcast line, being thrown across the space and then twisted back over itself to the starting-point, where it is in the right position for continuing the overcast line. The crosses being put in at the same time as the overcasting of the bars renders some forethought necessary to get each in at just the right time and place.

Another kind of filling can be seen in progress in fig. 122. The stitches used in it are overcast and buttonhole. With the help of this last-mentioned stitch patterns of all kinds can be carried out, for each succeeding row of the stitch can be worked into the heading of the last row, and in this way it is possible to build up any required shape. This figure is a working

225

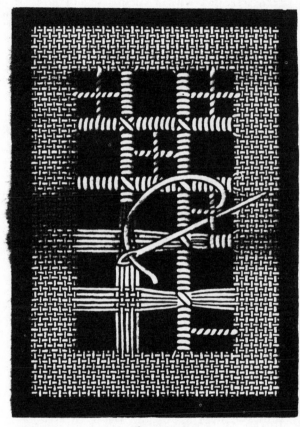

FIG. 121.

226

diagram of a piece of cut work of which the completed square with its surrounding decoration can be seen in fig. 34. After

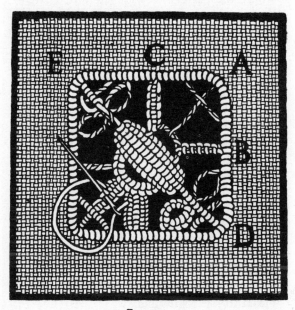

FIG. 122.

overcasting the raw edges a diagonal thread is thrown across (E D on plan), upon which the pattern shall be built up; the thread is taken once to and fro and

227

then twisted back again for a third crossing. Commence by overcasting the threads
from point D, and upon reaching the part
where the pattern is widened out, change
the stitch to an open buttonholing (as
shown on line B). It is worked openly
in this way in order to leave space for
another row of the same kind of stitching to be fitted in from the opposite side,
which is the next thing to be done.
Then an outer row of buttonhole stitch
is worked on each side of the central bar
and into the heading of the first row
of stitching; this is shown in progress
where the needle is at work. The entire
pattern is carried out in this way, first
laying down foundation threads in the
necessary places and then covering them
up with either overcasting or buttonhole
stitch as required. It is easily possible to
carry out flowers and all kinds of other
things sufficiently well to make them
pleasantly recognisable.

CHAPTER XI

EMBROIDERY WITH GOLD AND SILVER THREADS

Introduction—Materials—Precautions for the Prevention of Tarnish — Ancient Method of Couching—Its various Good Points—Description of Working Diagram—Working a Raised Bar—Examples of Patterns Employed in Old Work—Illustrations upon Draped Figures—Usual Method of Couching—Couching Patterns—Outline Work—Raised Work—The Use of Purls, Bullions, &c.

GOLD and silver threads have always played an important part in embroidered work, and are a most valuable addition to the worker's stock of materials, for they give a splendour and richness that is not obtainable in any other way. They have been utilised from the earliest times in both embroidery and weaving ; in scripture and other ancient historical writings there is abundant proof of this fact.

The earliest form of gold thread in use was the pure metal beaten into thin plates and then cut into long narrow strips ; that

229

it was sometimes rounded into wire form
is very probable. The first wire-drawing
machine is said to have been invented by
a workman at Nuremberg, but it was not
until two centuries later that the drawing-
mills were introduced into England.

Gold thread, similar to that we now
use, entwined about a silk one, is mentioned in a XIVth century Latin poem;
also, it is known that in the XIIIth century our English ladies prepared their
own gold thread before working it in, and
it was of the same type as ours, the gold
being spirally twisted round a thread of
silk or flax.[1]

To be a skilled worker with gold
thread needs considerable application and
practice. There is much variety in the
work, some branches of it being more
simple to manipulate than others. It is
desirable for all workers to understand
something of gold work, for it is frequently employed in conjunction with
other embroidery, as well as alone.
Fig. 123 shows a couched line of gold
thread outlining some silk embroidery,
which gives a pretty jewel-like effect of
something precious in a setting of gold.

[1] See Dr. Rock's "Textile Fabrics."

230

Gold embroidery may be divided roughly into three main classes, outline work, solid flat work, and raised work. Outline work is, as far as technique is concerned, one of the simplest forms of gold embroidery. The pattern is followed round with a gold cord or double thread of passing, fixed either visibly or invisibly with a couching stitch; the work needs but an interesting design and suitable background to be most

FIG. 123.

successful. Fig. 124 illustrates a portion of a design, carried out with gold cord upon a velvet ground, which has been further enriched by the addition of little applied white flowers. The raised work, and that which introduces the use of purls and bullions, is at once more complicated, and perhaps hardly as pleasing as the simpler flat work.

231

The method of applying the gold to

FIG. 124.

the material is usually by couching of

232

one form or another, for most of the threads are too inflexible to be stitched through. The ground, if it shows at all, is usually a rich stuff, such as velvet, satin, or silk, in order to be in keeping with the valuable thread. If the ground chosen is difficult to work upon, the embroidery is carried out upon linen, and the finished work afterwards applied to the ground. If both background and pattern are solidly embroidered, linen can be used as the permanent ground. It is usual to have two layers of material for working upon, for gold threads are heavy and require the support of the double ground. There are several advantages in this double material, as the old workers knew, for we find they commonly used two. The under-layer can be a strong linen, and the surface one silk, satin, or a fine linen, as required.

MATERIALS

A variety of metal threads are manufactured for embroidery purposes, and they are all obtainable in gold, silver, or imitations of these; aluminium thread has been made lately, and has the advantage

233

of being untarnishable, but its colour and
quality do not seem quite satisfactory, and
it is not popular. The imitation threads
are never worth the using; they tarnish to
a worse colour, and are more difficult in
manipulation; what goes by the name of
real gold, is silver or copper, plated with
the more valuable metal. The pure gold
thread is said not to be so practical as
this, being too brittle; but somehow or
other it was more successfully manufactured in the past than nowadays, for
some gold work six centuries old exhibits
beautifully bright threads.

The following list comprises the chief
threads used in this work:—

Passing. — This is a bright smooth
thread, resembling in appearance a gold
wire; it consists of a narrow flat strip
of gold spirally twisted round a silken
thread. It can be obtained in different
sizes, the finest qualities going by the
name of tambour. Most passing has to
be couched on to the material, but it
is possible to stitch in the tambour like
ordinary thread.

Purl.—This resembles a smooth round
hollow tube of metal, very pliable and
elastic; when pulled lengthways it is

234

found to be constructed like a closely
coiled spiral spring. It is manufactured
in lengths of about one yard, and for use
it is cut into small sections of any required
size with scissors or a knife. There are
several varieties of purl, namely, the
smooth, rough, check, and wire check.
The smooth has a bright polished appearance, which is obtained by a flat gold
wire being spun spirally round; the rough
has a duller and more yellow appearance,
which is owing to the wire having been
rounded; the check is bright and sparkling, and consists of the flattened wire
spun in a different way, so that parts of
it catch the light and sparkle; the wire
check is the same thing, but duller and
of a deeper yellow, owing again to its
being made of the round wire.

Bullion.—This is the name given to
the larger sizes of purl.

Pearl Purl.—This is manufactured in
the same spiral tube-like fashion as the
other purl, but the gold wire is previously hollowed out in this ∩ shape,
the convex side being the one exposed.
This, when spun round, has the appearance of a string of tiny gold beads. It
is frequently used as an outlining thread.

235

Various gold twists and cords can be obtained; they are composed of several threads twisted up in the usual cord fashion, each ply consisting of gold spun round a silk thread.

Plate is a flat strip of metal commonly about one-sixteenth of an inch wide; it can be obtained in different widths.

Spangles.—These are small variously shaped pieces of thin metal, usually pierced with a hole in the centre for fixing on to the material. They are frequently circular in shape, and either flat or slightly concave; the latter are the prettier. Many fancy shapes also are obtainable, but they are inclined to look tawdry, and suggestive of the panto-mime.

Cloth of Gold and Silver.—This is a fabric manufactured of silk, with gold or silver thread inwoven in the making. It is not now so much used as formerly, when it was in great request for robes of kings and other high dignitaries of church or state.

A special make of silk for couching down gold thread is obtainable in various colours. It is called horsetail or sewings, and is both fine and strong.

236

Padding for use in raised gold work is usually yellow, and for silver, white or grey. Yellow soft cotton, linen thread, or silk, are all used for the purpose.

Various precautions can and must be taken to keep the gold thread bright, for under unfavourable circumstances it rapidly assumes a bad colour; the silver thread is even more liable to tarnish than the gold, and it turns a worse colour, going black. There is a special paper manufactured to wrap threads in, and the stock supply should be kept in a tin or air-tight bottle; this is in order to protect the metal from damp, which is most injurious; to do this is a difficult matter in the English climate. Linen used for working upon, or as backing, is best unbleached, for sometimes the chemicals used in the bleaching process have a deleterious effect upon the gold; a piece of gold embroidery wrapped up in cotton wool for preservation has been found completely spoiled by some chemical in this wool, which proved more disastrous than exposure to air would have been. Gas, strong scents, handling (especially with hot hands), all have an evil effect, and so should be avoided as much as possible. Work even whilst in progress should be kept covered as much as is practicable, and should not be allowed to hang about; the quicker it is done the better. A piece of finished work can be polished up with a leather pad or a brush, similar to a housemaid's brush for silver-cleaning purposes; this of course, must be used with care.

ANCIENT METHOD OF COUCHING

Gold thread can be couched on to the material in two distinct ways, one of them in use at the present day, the other one that was commonly practised in the XIIIth and XIVth centuries. About the second half of the last-named century the earlier method was supplanted by the present one. Almost every example of early gold thread work exhibits this obsolete and ingenious method of couching. The Syon cope and the Jesse cope in the Victoria and Albert Museum may be mentioned as famous examples. M. Louis de Farcy[1] draws especial attention

[1] In *La Broderie du Onzième Siècle jusqu'à Nos Jours*.

238

to this beautiful method of working, to which he gives the name *point couché rentré ou retiré*, and strongly urges its revival; he points out many distinct advantages it has over the method now in use.

The durability is very great, owing to the couching thread being upon the reverse side, where it is protected from wear and tear, and being out of sight can be made strong and durable. If a thread is accidentally broken it does not necessarily give way along an entire line, as may easily happen in the present method. A proof of this point can be seen upon the beautiful Ascoli cope lately in the Victoria and Albert Museum, about which there has been so much discussion of late as to in what country it originated and who was the rightful owner. The early couching worked entirely over the background of the cope is in a state of perfect preservation; portions of the gold thread drapery have here and there been couched by the other method, the tying down threads have, in those parts, mostly disappeared, and the gold hangs loose and ragged upon the surface.

By the way in which it is worked, there results a particularly pleasing and even surface, agreeably varied by play of light and shade. Another advantage of the ancient method is that the completed work is very flexible; this point will appeal to those who have experienced the extreme stiffness of a large surface of ordinarily couched metal threads. Flexibility is an invaluable quality for any work destined, like copes and curtains, to hang in folds.

Representations of draperies upon figures are well expressed, for by the way in which they are worked there comes an indentation along the lines marking the folds; this emphasises them rather happily, and also breaks up the surface in a satisfactory manner.

Fig. 125 is a diagram that will aid in explaining the working, it gives both the front and the reverse side. This has been found to be the simplest and the most practical method of obtaining a result similar to the early examples; there is, however, no means other than examination of result whereby to get at this obsolete method. To all appearance there is upon the surface a kind of satin stitch worked in gold passing, the stitches carrying out some geometrical pattern, such as a chevron or lattice; but at

240

the back a linen thread is seen running to and fro in close parallel lines in the same direction as the surface thread, and at regular intervals encircled by the gold passing, just as if this was intended to couch down the linen thread.

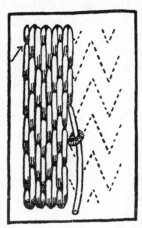

Front.   FIG. 125.   Back.

The ingenuity and satisfactoriness of the method must be admitted by all who give it a trial, and it is interesting to conjecture how it may have arisen. Possibly weaving suggested it to the embroiderers, for, take away the intervening material, and it is not unlike

241

woven work, and these two arts would very likely be the accomplishment of the same person. Perhaps the commonly used method of taking a coarse thread through to the back (see fig. 167) suggested it, for this is briefly the whole process.

In order to try the couching, a two-fold ground material must be firmly stretched in an embroidery frame, a strong linen underneath and a thinner closely woven one upon the upper side. Some fine gold passing and some strong linen thread, well waxed, are required to work with, also an embroidery needle with long eye and sharp point, the size, which is important, depending upon the threads in use; the needle has to pierce the two-fold ground material, making a hole only just large enough for the passage of a double gold thread.

If the linen has a regular even thread the drawn pattern shown in the diagram can be worked by counting the threads of the ground fabric, but if this is difficult or impossible, as in the case say of a twilled surface, a careful tracing must be made upon the linen; a beginner may find this the easier way in any case.

The end of the gold thread, which by

now, in readiness for working, will be
wound upon the bobbin or spindle, must be
passed through to the back at the starting-
point, the top left-hand corner in the
diagram. The linen thread secures it at
the back and then comes through to the
front upon the traced line exactly beneath
(see arrow on plan). It now encircles the
gold thread which the left hand draws out
rather tautly, and then returns by the
same hole to the back, pulling the metal
thread through with it. There is knack
in taking the gold thread only just through
and leaving the completed stitch straight
and flat upon the surface. The process
is now repeated, the linen thread coming
through to the front again upon the next
traced line, and so on. When the base
of the pattern is reached the gold thread
is taken through once upon that line, and
then commences a like journey upwards.

This practically explains the couching;
variety is obtained by change of pattern,
but the method of carrying it out is always
the same. Figs. 126, 127, and 128 show
three patterns taken from old examples
of this couching.

The difficulties in technique are easily
overcome; an important aid in this matter

243

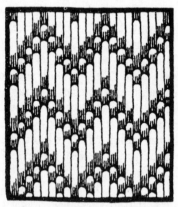

FIG. 126.

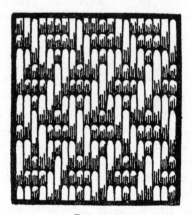

FIG. 127.

244

is the use of materials exactly right; this means needles and threads of the correct size, the ground composed of suitable fabrics, and properly strained in a frame. The aim in the working is to get each stitch perfectly flat and straight in its

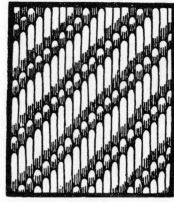

FIG. 128.

correct place in spite of the obstinacy of the metal thread; to avoid making the perforation larger than necessary, for this makes the work clumsy; to make each succeeding line lie closely beside the last one, for the surface must be of solid gold, and if the ground showed through in places it would impoverish the effect.

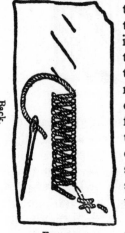

Front.

Back.

FIG. 129.

246

The direction of the couched thread is usually either vertical or horizontal, and it may be both of these in the same piece of work. The reason of this may be because it is worked by counting the threads of the fabric, or because the pattern is always treated as a diaper and placed upon the surface without regard to contour. The exception to this rule of direction is when the couching is taken along a stem or the narrow hem of a robe to form the border, or along a girdle, it then follows the direction of the band, this being evidently the most straightforward and satisfactory method to use for the purpose.

The *point couché rentré ou retiré* is an excellent

method to use for working a raised bar.
Fig. 129 shows the front and reverse sides
of a bar worked by it. The gold thread
comes cleanly through from the back of
the material instead of being clumsily
doubled upon the surface, and the durability is evidently great. The linen thread,
it will be seen, runs to and fro at the back,
at each turn securing the gold thread.

In fig. 130 this couching is to be seen
in use upon drapery. It is taken entirely
over the exterior surface of the cloak, and
upon the crown, sceptre, and model of
the church. The lines expressing the
folds of drapery are in this case shown by
the couching at these places being taken
in a different direction. Fine gold passing
is used for the couched thread, much finer
than can possibly be shown in the drawing,
and the pattern chosen for the couching
down is a chevron. The other parts of
the work are done with silk thread in a
fine chain or split stitch. The play of
light upon the varied surface of the
golden cloak is very beautiful; the
drawing of the figure is perhaps primitive,
and, regarded from the draughtsman's
point of view, somewhat ludicrous; it is
however sufficiently good to express all

247

Embroidery
with Gold
and Silver
Threads

248   FIG. 130.

that its author intended, and there is something very human in this dignified little king who would not have you forget that he founded a church. The king who is personified here is Edward the Confessor, so the church is Westminster Abbey, of which he was the founder.

The Madonna and child forming the frontispiece of the work is another example of this couching. The method of expressing the folds of drapery is slightly different from that employed upon the king's robes. All drapery carried out in this stitch is

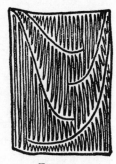

FIG. 131.

worked in somewhat the same fashion, that is, the couching running to and fro between the lines marks each fold as roughly shown at fig. 131. This method leaves an indented line to express the drapery, which is a more satisfactory way than a simple line of dark colour worked over the gold, as in more modern work. The indented line is often further emphasised by a line of dark silk stitched

249

along it, which is done in this case.
The figures are taken from the Jesse cope
in the Victoria and Albert Museum;[1]
this vestment, with its red silk background
and its finely coloured and drawn ancestors
of Christ posed amongst encircling vine
branches, is a most beautiful, though
sadly mutilated, example of XIIIth century design and workmanship.

MODERN METHOD OF COUCHING

In the usual form of couching the gold
thread is attached to the material by
fine strong silk. The thread is fastened
down as a rule two-fold, sometimes even
three-fold; this method is both quicker
and more effective than couching each
thread separately. As the couching thread
is necessarily in evidence, decorative use is
often made of it as well as practical; the
stitches, for instance, may be planned so
as to carry out some pattern (see fig. 132)
instead of being put down at random.
There is no limit to the variety of the
patterns that can be devised in this
way.

Decorative use can be made of the colour

[1] No. 175, 1889.

of the couching thread; a hot colour warms the tone of the gold and a cool one does the

reverse ; and the more contrasting the colour the more it is in evidence.

The gold thread may be couched solidly in straight lines, as the above figure shows, or it may be arranged in wavy lines either close

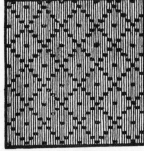

FIG. 132.

or open, as in fig. 133. The thread is waved by bending it round the pointed end of a piercer just before fixing down. This waving line is particularly suitable for the gold thread, since the slight change in direction allows

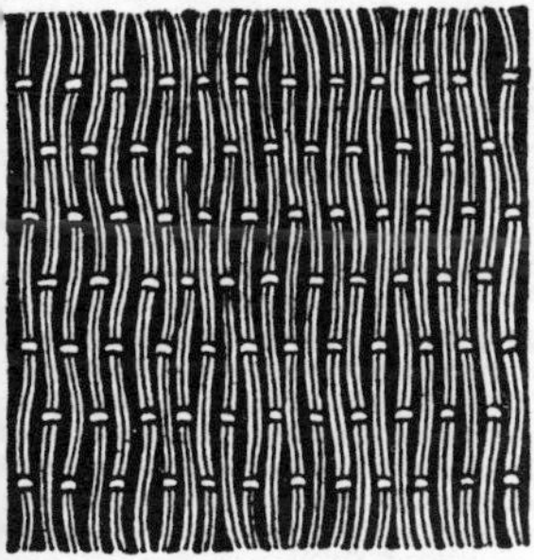

FIG. 133.

the light to play upon the metal very prettily. For this reason gold is often

251

couched solidly in circular or shell form over a ground. In gold embroidery, therefore, the direction of the thread is a specially important matter.

At the end of a line a technical difficulty sometimes arises in the turning of the thread, which is apt to be clumsy. This difficulty is overcome in various ways; the most usual is to return the doubled thread as neatly as possible and continue the next line; another is to cut the

FIG. 134.

thread sharp off, secure it close to the end with a double stitch, and recommence in like fashion; the thread can sometimes be passed through to the back and brought up in position for working the next line. The fine point of a leaf may present difficulties in the same way; sometimes one of the two threads is temporarily let slip and the point completed with the single one, the left thread being picked up upon the return (see fig. 134). For such occasions as this it is more practical

252

to wind the two threads of passing upon
separate bobbins, and bring them together
at the working. Another way of over-
coming the point difficulty is shown at
fig. 135.

RAISED WORK

The couched gold threads may be raised
in parts by means of some kind of padding
interposed between it and the ground. They
are very effective so
treated, since the
raised metal catches
and reflects the
light in a pleasing
manner. This rais-

FIG. 135.

ing of the thread, however, has been
carried to such extremes as to resemble
goldsmith's work rather than embroidery,
and it is then hardly in good taste.

A simple method of raising the gold
is to lay down lines of string at stated
intervals over the ground. The well-
known form called basket stitch is done
in this way; fig. 136 illustrates this stitch,
a part of the square is left unworked in
order to expose the under-layer of string.
To carry out the diagram—First couch

down the lines of string at regular intervals over the surface, then commence laying on the gold by carrying a doubled thread of passing over two bars of string, and there fixing it down to the material, then over two more and fixing it down again, and so on to the end of the line. This is exactly repeated for a second line of passing, then, for the next two lines, commence by carrying the passing for the first stitch over one bar only, and for the remainder of the line over the two as before. This process repeated makes the wicker-like pattern so frequently seen in gold work. It can be used as a filling or as a border. It is evident that with the same arrangement of strings many other patterns could be carried out by varying the points of couching down.

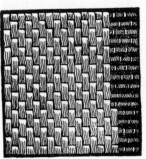

FIG. 136.

Another way in which string is used for padding the gold is illustrated in fig. 137. The pattern, which in the first part

254

is two diamond shapes and a border line, is laid down in string. The doubled gold thread is then taken horizontally to and fro in close parallel lines over the part to be worked, and fixed by couching stitches at necessary intervals; wherever else these stitches may be put, one must always be placed upon each side of a raised line to make it sharp and clear. Other kinds of padding are used in this method of work; for instance, a lozenge shape may be stuffed with layers of soft cotton, as shown in the second

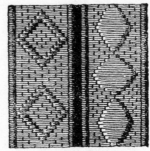

FIG. 137.

part of this same diagram. Sometimes most complicated patterns are laid down in string and covered with gold thread in this way, *e.g.*:—fig. 138 shows an interlacing pattern taken from the border of an orphrey upon a XVth century chasuble.

255

THE USE OF FANCY GOLD THREADS

A cursory glance must be given to the use of purls and other fancy threads, but these are mostly used nowadays for badges on uniforms, or for masonic purposes, and are carried out by the trade. These

FIG. 138.

threads, when tarnished, are very diffi-cult to clean, they easily turn a bad colour and catch the dust, and for real embroi-dery purposes are not as satisfactory as the plainer threads.

Purl and bullion must be cut very accurately into pieces of the required size, and attached to the material as a bead would be. The metal must be as little

256

as possible touched with the fingers; the
cut pieces can be placed upon a tray lined
with some soft springy substance, such as
felt, in order to be easily picked up with
the point of the needle, and they can
be adjusted to their right position upon
the work by the aid of the flat end of the
piercer; unnecessary handling may be
avoided in this way.

These threads, laid over padding either
straight across or at an angle, may be used
for the stems or petals of conventional
flowers. The various kinds, dull, bright,
and check, may perhaps be used in succession.

Plate is frequently taken to and fro over
the same kind of forms over a prepared
padding, being caught down by a stitch
on each side by a method the French call
le guipé. It needs skill and practice to
do this well. Crinkled plate used to be
couched on to work, but now is not much
used in this way.

Pearl purl is most often seen outlining
a form filled in with the other threads;
an enlarged example of this thread lies
vertically down the centre of fig. 139,
the end of it is pulled out, in order to
show the formation of the thread.

257

Spangles are usually sewn down separately; they may be attached by stitches from the centre outwards or by the thread being passed through a piece of purl and then returning to the back

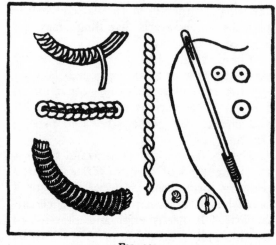

FIG. 139.

through the hole in the centre of the spangle. Fig. 139 illustrates another way of using these spangles to form a long tail shape. Here again they are attached with the help of pieces of purl. In the same figure are given some illustrations of the use of the fancy threads;

258

to learn more about them the student should examine XVIth to XVIIIth century gold work during which period they were in popular use.

CHAPTER XII

LETTERING, HERALDRY, AND EMBLEMS

The Uses of Lettering—Marking—Monograms—Heraldry—Emblems.

LETTERING of one kind or another is frequently in request. It is useful for inscriptions, verses, names attached to figures, the signing and dating of work, and for the more ordinary purposes of marking linen and so forth. Signed and dated work has peculiar attractiveness: it can be placed amidst definite historical associations: an authenticated piece of embroidery, say of the reign of King Richard Cœur de Lion, Queen Anne, or George III., would be an historical document and a standard to gauge the period of any uninscribed examples. Although few of us are likely to possess treasures of the XIIIth century, signed and dated

259

pieces of our great - grandmothers' embroideries are interesting personal land-
marks in family history, so for this reason,
amongst others, unostentatious marks of
identification are by no means out of
place. Descriptive names or verses are
also a means of amplifying the story and
so enlivening our curiosity.

Lettering can answer a further purpose

FIG. 140.

still; it can enrich the design, for, if
rightly chosen and employed, letters are
very decorative. They may be seen forming a border to a piece of work. The
three letters in fig. 140 were taken from
an XIth century embroidered cope, which
has a fine inscription running round the
entire lower margin.[1] The names of the

[1] This cope is full of interest in every detail. See
M. Louis de Farcy, *La Broderie du Onzième Siècle
jusqu'à Nos Jours*. Plate II.

260

saints and martyrs standing in rows in the columned arcades, affected at certain periods, are sometimes inscribed in the

FIG. 141.

mouldings of the arches above them or along the base; kneeling donors can be seen naïvely presenting a little scroll inscribed with prayers, and many other

261

interesting uses of lettering might be recalled. The names St. Luke and St. John, shown in fig. 141, are taken from a beautiful embroidered example of Gothic lettering.

Illuminated manuscripts supply fine examples of initial letters and writing. A visit to the show-cases in the King's Library at the British Museum will be of great interest to the student; the illustrations also to be seen there, the beautifully composed and coloured figure-subjects, would be equally suitable for carrying out in embroidery; indeed it is very probable that many of the figure compositions on the old copes and chasubles were derived from such a source. Fig. 142 gives as an example of an alphabet one taken from a Benedictionale of late XVth century date.

A practical purpose to which lettering is often put is the marking of linen. To learn how to do this used to be a recognised part of a girl's education, and was one of the objects of the sampler. Marking can be anything from a simple cross-stitch initial to an elaborately worked monogram. For simple work the corner to be marked can be tacked upon *toile*

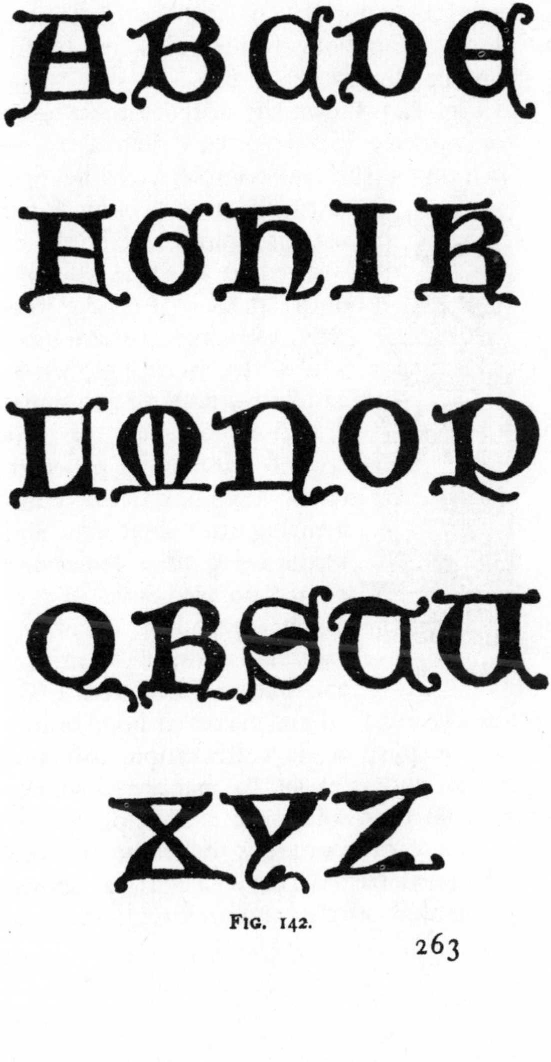

ABCDE

FGHIK

LMNOP

QRSTU

XYZ

FIG. 142.

cirée, a material not unlike Amerıcan cloth. Tambour frames also are useful for this purpose.

Fig. 143 shows the stitches most used for working simple letters such as those seen upon the old samplers. The first

is cross stitch, which for marking purposes should be worked so as to be alike on both sides. To do this requires some forethought whilst the work progresses, and necessitates an occasional doubling of one of the crossed stitches, in order to reach the point for commencing the next one and at the same time preserving a cross on each side.

The second stitch in the diagram shows a square on one side and is a cross upon the reverse. This makes a good stitch for the purpose, is quite simple to manipulate, and is easier to manage than the cross on both sides.

Fig. 143.

The third example is made use of when a larger letter is required. It is known as blanket stitch, and is used for the

264

marking of such things. It may be further completed by a neat back stitch just fitting along the outside edges of the other stitches.

Many embroidery stitches are suitable for marking pur-poses, such as satin, chain, stem, back, rope, basket, and others. The Oriental stitch which carries out the letter in fig. 144 is a good one when both sides can be seen, for though these are quite differ-ent, it is presentable upon either. The diagram shows the appearance of the stitch on the front and on the back.

FIG. 144.

A simple initial letter may be made interesting by enriching the ground be-hind it with some form of diaper pattern-ing. An example of this is shown in fig. 145. The letter could be worked in a plain satin stitch over a padding of threads, and the pattern on the ground

265

in a darning stitch and French knots, or in any other suitable way.

A monogram carried out in embroidery can be a very pretty thing; there is scope in it for ingenuity both of design and of stitching. The letters may be decorated and tied up with a floral spray, strap work or a combination of several *motifs.* Fig. 146 shows a monogram composed of the letters I. G. ornamented and bound together by a ribbon-like interlacing band. The letters are worked in a raised satin stitch, and a running stitch in another colour threads in and out down the centre of each letter. The outline is stem stitch in a darker colour. The band is outlined on both sides with an overcast stitch, which always makes a particularly neat edging for anything of this sort. The centre is filled with a row of French knots, the tassels are worked in close lines of stem stitch,

FIG. 145.

266

and the petals of the small flowers in

FIG. 146.

satin stitch, finished off with a French knot at the centre.

267

Another mark of proprietorship and origin was the shield of arms of the owner, which introduces the subject of heraldry. A shield executed with the needle is often seen, and looks particularly rich. Heraldry is an intricate science, full of pitfalls for the unwary, and demands an earnest study of its complex rules and regulations. Every one should know at least some fine examples of great national shields such as the Lions of England, the Fleur de Lys of France, and the Imperial Eagle. Examples of shields surmounted by helmets and crests with quaint and flowing mantling are to be seen in all kinds of art work.

Various stitches and methods specially lend themselves to the expression of heraldry. Those which, like cross stitch, impose a certain simplicity, are very good. Another suitable medium is applied work, of which an illustration can be seen on page 95. Gold and silver thread are very useful here, and look exceptionally rich when couched in the XIIIth century method. Fig. 147 is an embroidered coat of arms dated the first half of the XIVth century. It is executed almost entirely in the *point couché*

rentré ou retiré. The arms are those of the
Clinton and Leyburne families—*argent,*

FIG. 147.

6 *cross crosslets fitchée* 3, 2 *and* 1 *on a chief
azure, two mullets or.*

In designing heraldic work care must
be taken to introduce no debased forms
such as were current after the XVth

269

century. The XIIIth and XIVth centuries are the periods considered best for the study of this subject. Heraldry sometimes adds historic interest to embroideries; owners or donors may be

FIG. 148.

traced by their coat of arms appearing upon some part of the work.

Allied to heraldry and marking are a number of decorative objects that have acquired peculiar traditional significance of an emblematic or symbolical nature, hard

270

to define. The Cross of Christianity may be instanced, the olive branch of peace, the mirror of truth, and the snake of eternity. The name of a saint is frequently declared by an emblem accompanying the figure. In appropriate surroundings emblems may often be used effectively. For knowledge about these things the student must go to various books that deal with the special subject. Fig. 148 is an illustration of the well-known emblem, the Pelican in her piety.

CHAPTER XIII

THE GARNITURE OF WORK

Finishing off—Making up—Edges—Use of Cordmaking Appliance—Cord Twisted by Hand—Knotted Cord—Fringes—Tassels—Knots.

WHEN the embroidery is completed, the making up, the addition of tasteful finishing touches, and such things as fringes, tassels, and linings, must all be considered. These will, if judiciously made use of, give a distinction and character to the work that might be missed if due care and thought were not expended upon such details

271

This part of the work might be compared to the garnishing of a boiled fowl with lemon and parsley, a minor detail, but a very effective one.

It is possible, by the help of such expedients, to emphasise certain colours and bring out points of the design, as well as to give completeness and finish. Such things as fringes, cords, and tassels are often more satisfactory when made by the worker and with materials like those used in the embroidery, for such will be more likely to be in keeping with the character of the rest, and to be more interesting in detail. In the finishing off the same taste and neatness of execution is required as in the embroidery. Good work can be very much marred in the making up; on the other hand, a little extra interest added on a part not often seen renders it doubly valuable.

The mounting of certain things should not be attempted at home; boxes should be handed over to the cabinetmaker, books to the bookbinder, and so on, for it is not possible for any one not an expert to do these things properly, and even good work can look poor if badly set.

The question how to appropriately

finish off an edge often arises; let it be hem stitched rather than plain hemmed; or a narrow line of drawn thread work may be inserted, for an open-work border is frequently a set-off to the rest of the embroidery. If a binding is placed over the edge this can be fixed with a pretty stitch, or the stitch alone can bind the edge, one such as buttonhole, overcast, or that shown in fig. 76. With some stitches the edge of the material can be rolled over a piping cord and the stitch worked over the thus emphasised margin.

The difficulty of procuring cord suitable for use with embroidered work makes the appliance illustrated at fig. 149 a useful possession.[1] The cords made upon this wheel can be of any thickness, according to the number of plies and the substance in each. Different colours and materials can be twisted up together, such as a gold and silk thread.

To make a three-plied cord, cut three equal lengths of thread rather longer than the required cord is to be, as it shortens

[1] This will be found described in detail in Chapter II. There is an interesting drawing of a neat little machine, similar to this, but worked by cogwheels, in *L'Art du Brodeur*, by Germain de St. Aubin (1770).

273

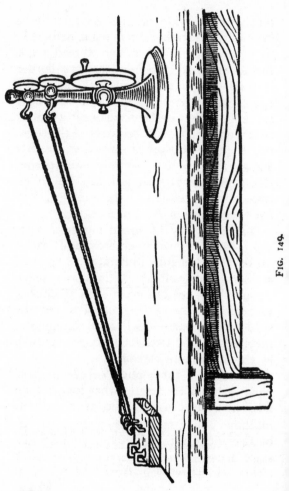

FIG. 149.

in the twisting. Make a loop at each
end of the thread, or, better still, attach
tiny metal rings at the ends. Hook the
threads in position as shown in the
diagram, and place the instrument far
enough from the clamped block of wood
to make the threads that are stretched
between quite taut. Now commence the
twisting by turning the large wheel
quickly with an even motion in the
direction that continues to twist up the
threads, keeping the left hand on the
instrument to steady it, for it gradually
slides towards the block as the twisting
continues. When corkscrew-like knots
begin to come in the threads, stop re-
volving the wheel, unhook the two outer
threads and place them both on the
central hooks together with the third
thread, keeping them taut during the
process. Revolve the large wheel again,
in the direction opposite to that in which
it has been working, and continue turning
until the cord is tightly twisted up. It is
now made, and can be removed from the
machine. The second twisting had better
be over-done rather than not sufficiently,
since if over-twisted the cord rights itself
upon being removed from the machine.

A two-ply cord is made in like manner,
by using first the two outer hooks only,
and then placing both threads together on
the central hooks.

There is a simple way of making this
cord without the help of any instrument,
but it is not possible to get the perfect
result that the machine gives. It is most
easily carried out by two persons, though
one can do it. In order to make a
two-plied cord, by hand, take a thread
rather more than twice the length of
the required cord. Let each worker
take an end of the thread in the right
hand and commence to twist it between
the thumb and finger, each working in
direction opposite to the other and keeping
the thread at tension. When twisted as
much as possible without getting corkscrew-like knots in the thread, the cord
must be doubled in half by holding it
at the centre and bringing together the
two ends, which are then knotted. During
the entire process the thread must be
kept under tension. If one end of the
cord is now let go it should immediately
twist itself up tight, and remain in
that position. If any small knots form
during the process run the cord sharply

276

through the fingers once or twice to
straighten it out.

Another pretty kind of cord is a
knotted one. It is made in the hand
in most primitive fashion by using the
two first fingers as crochet hooks. The
thread used for making it should be

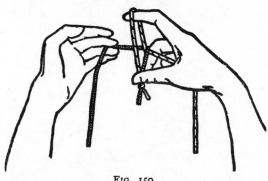

FIG. 150.

stout and firm. To commence making
the cord, knot two pieces of thread
together and place the threads in position
as shown in fig. 150. The next step is
shown in fig. 151, which is the index
finger of the left hand bringing the darker
thread through the loop. Fig. 152 shows
this thread looped on the finger, the cord
held in the left hand instead of the right,

277

and the right hand in process of drawing
the lighter thread, which was the last

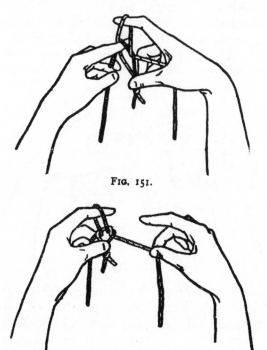

FIG. 151.

FIG. 152.

loop, tight. The next move, fig. 153,
shows the right-hand first finger making
the new loop with the lighter thread, and
278

fig. 154 shows the loop on the finger, the cord passed over to be held in the

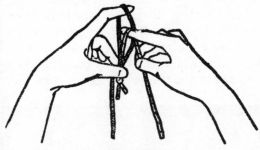

FIG. 153.

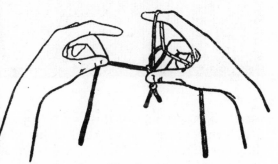

FIG. 154.

right hand again, and the left hand this time pulling the last loop tight. Continue making the cord by following out the last four positions consecutively.

279

A very usual finish to an edge is a fringe. This can be made either by fraying out the material or by adding a detached fringe, either knotting it in or attaching it in some other way. If the fringe is to be a frayed-out one, the best way to do it is to first draw out a few warp threads where the head of the fringe is to come, then hem

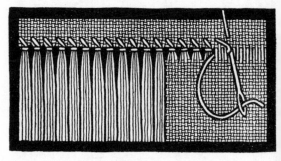

FIG. 155.

stitch the upper edge of this, see the right-hand end of fig. 155; this makes the heading of the fringe secure, after which the remainder of the warp threads can be withdrawn. When fringing a square in this fashion, it is well to save some of the frayings out to knot in at the four corners where otherwise there would be gaps.

To knot an added fringe into the

border is a very simple matter. Begin
by cutting the threads that are to compose it all to one length, about double
that of the required fringe. Take a few
together to form a bunch and double it
in half. With a stiletto make a hole
near the edge of the material; then bring
from the back a crochet hook through
this hole, and draw the loop formed by
the doubling of the bunch a little way

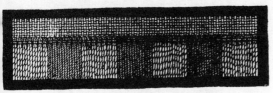

FIG. 156.

through, then take the ends of the bunch
through the loop and draw them tight in
order to make the knotting firm.

There are many ways of patterning a
plain fringe, sometimes a change of colour
in the knotted-in threads is sufficient, as
shown in fig. 156. Another very usual
way is to divide the bunches and refasten
them together in some way to form a
pattern. Fig. 157 is an example of this;
they may be either knotted together, as

281

in the first half of the diagram, or bound with thread as in the second half, the needle reaching the required places by running in zigzag fashion up the thread and down again.

A simple fringe can be made of strands twisted together, as in the first half of fig. 158. This is made upon the same

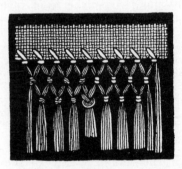

FIG. 157.

principle as the twisted cord already described. About three threads of the fringe are twisted up tight, and an adjoining three treated in the same fashion. These threes are then twisted together in the direction opposite to that which has just been used, and thus are securely locked together. The ends of the completed fringe may require a little trimming

282

off to make all of an equal length. The
second half of the diagram shows a durable and simple fringe made by a close
series of knots down the thread.

Fig. 159 suggests two methods by
which a stitching of coloured thread near

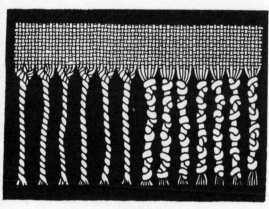

FIG. 158.

the margin can help to decorate a plain
fringed edge.

A row of tassels makes a pretty finish
to various things. Complicated tassel-
making requires a professional hand;
even a simple tassel requires making
properly. The first proceeding is to
wind some thread round a piece of card-

283

board, which should be a little wider
than the tassel is to be long ; then double
a piece of the same thread and thread the
two ends into a needle, thus leaving a
loop at the usual knot end.   Slip the
needle through the centre of the wound

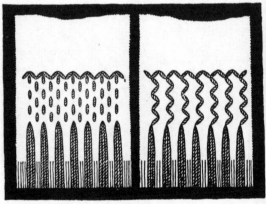

Fig. 159.

thread close to the cardboard, then
through the loop and draw the thread
tight ; this will bind the threads securely
at that point.   They can then be cut
exactly opposite this on the other side,
which will release the cardboard.   Give
the binding thread another tightening
pull, and then take the needle and thread

straight through the centre, as shown in
fig. 160, and fasten it off with a good
knot. This knot will be in the ball part
of the tassel and will help to make it
round. Next, double the tassel into
shape ready for the collar. Thread the
needle as before and make the thread

FIG. 160.

encircle the tassel, as shown in the second
figure in the diagram, drawing the thread
quite tight, and, if necessary, winding
it several times round the neck of the
tassel until the collar is of sufficient width,
then take the needle and thread straight
through the centre, bringing it out at the
top, where it can be made use of to fix
the tassel in its place upon the work

With sharp scissors trim the edge of the
tassel which now is complete. The ball
part can be further decorated by covering
it with an open network of stitches in some
contrasting colour; buttonhole and various
lace stitches can be used for the purpose.

KNOTS

Knots, which can be very pretty, are
at times required in embroidery; anything that requires a fastening may give
an opportunity for some pretty interlacing strap work or knotting. Also knots
may be practically useful in both weaving
and embroidery, for sometimes a finishing
thread must be knotted on to a new one,
since there may be no opportunity of
making a firm commencement with the
aid of the material.

The knot shown in fig. 161 is called
the girdle knot; it might be made use
of in many other ways. To carry it
out, make a loop with one end of the
cord and hold it between the left finger
and thumb, the looped part being towards
the right, and the end that points downwards to the left passing over the other
end. Take up the other piece of cord,
pass it diagonally across the surface of
286

the loop, commencing from the right-hand lower side, then round under one end and over the other, then up into the loop from underneath, over its own end that crosses the loop there, and then out under the loop at the top right-hand corner.

The Chinese knot, which is used for a sailor's collar, is shown in fig. 162. The

FIG. 161.

looped end can be left as large as necessary. To work it the first part of the knot is laid in position on the table, commencing at point A; for the latter part (from point C) the thread is interlaced through to the finish. It can then be pulled tight, taking care in the drawing-together process that the various loops are adjusted in right position.

287

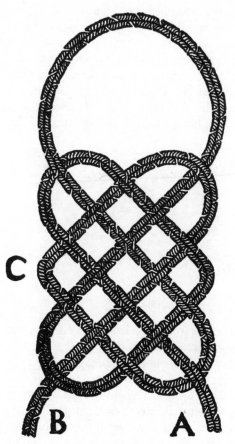

Fig. 162.

Another ornamental knot is shown at
fig. 163. To make it—Form a loop
and hold it between the left thumb and
finger, the loop pointing to the right, the
longer end pointing upwards and passing
over the end that points downwards. Take
hold of the end pointing upwards, pass
it perpendicularly downwards across the

FIG. 163.

surface of the loop, then round under the
other end, up over its own end, under the
side of the loop, over its own end that
lies across the loop, and out under the
loop at the right-hand end. Pull as
tight as required. All these knots may
be made of double cord by running a
second through, following the lead of
the first, just before tightening up the
knot. The one last described may be

289

made of doubled cord from the commencement, the looped end being used as
the working end : the knot will then finish

FIG. 164.

off with a loop at one end, which can be
used as a loop or cut if required.

Fig. 164 is an example of a pretty
piece of interlacing strap work attached
to a fastening.

The weavers' knot (fig. 165) is useful
for practical purposes in both weaving

290

and embroidery; this knot is univer-
sally employed by the cotton weavers
when the warp breaks. It is made as
follows—Place the two ends that are to
be knotted together between the thumb
and first finger of the left hand in such a
way that they cross each other at right
angles, the end that points towards the
left passing under the one pointing
towards the right. Pass the long end

FIG. 165.

of thread that hangs down towards the
right, and which is the newly attaching
piece, over the thumb, round the back of
the end pointing to the left in front of
the other end, and let it hang down again
towards the right, holding the loop thus
made between the thumb and finger;
then pass the end pointing towards the
right down through this loop and out on
the opposite side. To draw the knot tight,
pull the end which hangs down towards
the right, which will tighten the loop and
so complete the knot.

291

The reef knot (fig. 166) is another useful one, and it has this advantage over the weaver's knot, that both short ends

Fig. 166.

return parallel to the long ones instead of going off at an angle; this makes it neater for some purposes.

CHAPTER XIV

PRACTICAL DIRECTIONS

Transferring Patterns—Paste for Embroidery Purposes—Protection and Preservation of Work—Washing Embroidery—Prevention and Cure of Puckered Work—Points about the Thread—Dressing the Frame.

THE best method of getting the pattern on to the material is to draw it on directly with a brush; since this, however, is not always possible, other ways of doing it can be employed.

The pattern can be transferred to the background by a process called pouncing. To do this fix some tracing-paper over

292

the design and carefully take the outline; a good margin of plain paper
should be left round the outside in order
to prevent any of the pounce getting
accidentally rubbed on to the embroidery.
The next process is the perforation of the
pattern. Lay the tracing upon some substance of the nature of thick felt, then
with a pricker or a needle, held in an
upright position, pierce tiny holes all
round the outline of the pattern, very
close together. This completed, attach
the perforated tracing securely to the
material, the smooth side of the perforations towards the stuff. Both material
and tracing paper may be fixed to a board
with drawing pins. Next, rub the pounce,
which consists of finely powdered charcoal
or of white chalk, lightly over the perforated parts with a soft pad, keeping the
rubbing always in the same direction; once
or twice at the most over the surface is
quite sufficient, often too much is rubbed
through, which afterwards is only in the
way. The pad, first dipped into the
pounce, is rubbed preparatorily upon
some paper to remove the superfluous
powder, and then upon the actual work.
Carefully remove the tracing-paper; there

should now be visible upon the surface of the material, in charcoal dust, a perfectly clear reproduction of the pattern. Should, however, the impression be blurred, it is quite easy to flick everything away with a duster and repeat the process. The causes of failure would most probably be that the perforations were too large or too far apart, or that there was some movement of either paper or material during the process. It is necessary for the pattern to be permanently fixed upon the ground material; blow lightly to remove any superfluous powder, then, with a brush dipped in light red oil-paint moistened with turpentine, trace a fine clear line over the powdered pattern. When this is dry, what is left of the charcoal can be lightly dusted away. Red is in most cases a good colour to use for tracing purposes, for if by chance any tracing should show or come off on the thread it will be a clean-looking colour, and one comparatively easily removed in any after cleaning.

Red or blue carbonised paper is used for tracing patterns; it is not a good medium though it may be an expeditious one. If it is used, an after painting over the outline will make the marking permanent.

When pouncing or painting is difficult, a method of indicating the pattern upon the stuff is to trace the design on tissue paper, and tack it to the ground material with cotton, the stitching of which should follow the outline of the design, and be kept as much as possible upon the front. The thin paper is then torn away, and there will be some suggestion of pattern left upon the material.

Transparent ground stuffs need only be laid upon the pattern; then the tracing can be taken directly on the stuff.

Paste is sometimes in request for embroidery purposes; the following is a good recipe—Pour rather less than half a pint of cold water into a saucepan, add to this a piece of carpenter's glue about the size of a small filbert and place it on the fire to heat. Put three teaspoonfuls of flour into a basin, and with cold water mix to a smooth paste; when the water in the saucepan boils add it to the paste, stirring well all the time; then place the mixture in the saucepan and boil for about two minutes. When cold it is ready for use. It may be required as a preservative; for instance, canvas work when finished can have a thin coating of

paste rubbed over the back in order to preserve the stitches from giving or running ;
when the work is to be used for such
things as furniture coverings this may be
a good thing to do. Applied work is
sometimes pasted on to its new ground,
and a backing may be fixed to the surface
material by paste. The more all this can
be avoided the better, for its tendency is to
give a stiff mechanical look to work ; professional people, however, are rather fond
of the paste pot. Paste, if used, must be
of the right kind, or it will do more harm
than good. It should be very fresh, and
have no acid in its ingredients, of which
gum arabic must not be one if any after
stitching has to take place through the
stuff, for gum makes it hard and less pene-
trable. The paste must be applied and
allowed to dry thoroughly before the
work is removed from the frame. A
finger makes a good brush for the purpose.
The paste should be put on as thinly and
evenly as possible, care being taken not
to rub on the cross of the material, since
this might stretch it unevenly.

Shoemakers' paste is easily procured,
and can be used for embroidery purposes. This is made from rye flour, and

is very strong. It is harmless if perfectly fresh.

A good many things go to the keeping of work fresh and orderly, which is a very important matter. The work must be kept carefully covered up when not in use; finished parts can sometimes be covered whilst the work is going on, for the covering is easily raised when comparison with the part in progress is necessary. The work should have some protection if the hand rests on it; the worker should wear a white apron with sleeves. The worker's hand should be cool, dry, and smooth; hot hands should frequently be washed. The use of pumice stone cures slight roughness, but fine work cannot be attempted if the fingers are for any reason constantly rough. Wools and silks need a case to keep them orderly and clean. The best way to preserve valuable embroidery is to frame it, which, of course, is not always practicable, but it is a sure safeguard against moth and dust.

For washing embroidery special soap should be procured. It is not well to use any ordinary soap, for this may contain alkali, which would injure the colours in the work. Dissolve the soap in boiling water,

297

and add cold to make it just warm and of
the required strength. Immerse the embroidery in the lather thus made, and
work it about gently, avoiding any friction.
When clean, rinse first in warm water, afterwards in cold, to which a little salt may
be added. The water must be squeezed
out carefully and the material quickly
dried. If ironing is necessary it must be
done on the wrong side, but if the work
can be pinned out on a board to dry, and
in this way stretched and smoothed without
any ironing, so much the better, for the
embroidery will not be flattened at all.
Another way of ironing embroidery that
is not harmful is to do it from underneath
while some one holds out the material.

It is easy to prevent the puckering of
work when it is carried out in the frame;
there is, however, no necessity for it to
occur in hand work. Certain stitches are
more inclined to draw up the material
than others, and extra care has to be
taken in working upon the cross of the
fabric. The work should be held in
convex fashion over the fingers of the
left hand. Weights are occasionally
attached to the corners of the work to
prevent any unconscious drawing of it up.

There are remedies for the cure of slightly puckered work. Place on a drawing-board some clean blotting-paper, damp it evenly over with a wet handkerchief, and then lay the work, right side up, upon it. Fix the work down to the board with drawing-pins, inserted at regular short intervals round the edge, endeavouring during the process to stretch the material to its original shape. This needs doing carefully, for it is quite possible to stretch it to a wrong shape, and it will remain as now pinned out. Next, lay some white paper or a handkerchief upon the surface of the work, and then place upon it a flat weight that presses equally on every part of the embroidery. Leave it undisturbed for a night, and the puckering will probably be cured. Work, if not puckered, may be improved by going through this process, which practically amounts to a mild ironing, but without any injurious effects.

There are various points about the thread that should be known. To commence a new thread run a few stitches in the material upon the right side upon a part that will afterwards be covered by the working. This is a better way than a

299

fastening on the wrong side, for it is both neater and more secure. A knot made at the beginning is fairly safe, but it is undesirable for several reasons. The needleful should not be lengthy lest it gets worn before it is all worked in. With some threads it is important to thread only the proper end into the eye of the needle, since one way they will work in roughly and the other way smoothly. An end of a coarse thread can be taken through to the back of the material by the help of a fine one; the fine thread is brought through from the back by the needle, it then encircles the coarse one, and returns to the back by the same hole, pulling the coarse thread with it, as in process in fig. 167. Taking it through by the aid of a thick needle

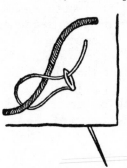

FIG. 167.

would make too large a hole. Thread can be knotted into the eye of the needle if for any reason it is required to be quite safe from accidental unthreading. The neatest way of doing this is to pass the

300

needle through the centre of the thread
and draw it tight; this is a useful trick
for any unskilled worker with needles and
thread, for re-threading also may be a difficulty. When work has to be unpicked
it is better to cut the threads rather
than do any drawing out, for they are in
any case unfit for further use, and this
method wears the material less; a beginner must not shirk unpicking if first-
rate results are to be obtained.

FRAME WORK

Certain stitches and methods of work
cannot be carried out except with the help
of a frame, others are hand stitches, and
some few can be worked either way. Work
done in a frame takes longer than that
done by hand, and is rather more fatiguing.
Each method has its advantages; in the
frame it is perhaps easier to get good
technique, for difficulties such as puckering
the material, irregular stitching, and so
on, are more easily avoided, also it is
more possible to see the effect of the
whole whilst the part progresses. In frame
work a thimble is required for each hand,
for one pushes the needle through from
above and one from below. It is a rest to

301

be able to reverse the hands, so both should
be equally dexterous in either position.

To dress the frame correctly is an important preliminary, for unless done well
the effect of much after labour may be
spoiled. In the chapter upon tools and
appliances in fig. 9 is shown a piece of
linen stretched in the frame ready for
commencing work.

The square of material that is seen to
be inserted in the centre of the stretched
linen is to show how a very small piece or
a portion of a large surface could be
stretched in the same sized frame. A
corner may require marking or a small
detail of embroidery carrying out upon it.
A portion is cut out of the centre of the
stretched linen, and the piece or part of
the material to be worked stitched securely
to it, as illustrated in the diagram. The
remainder of the material, if there is any,
can be folded up and pinned out of the
way over the rollers.

To return to the dressing of the frame
—the linen to be stretched, before being
fixed in place, must be hemmed or herring-
boned down at the top and base and then
sewn with overcast stitches to the webbings, inclining during the process to

pucker the webbing rather than the
material. The side pieces can now be put
through the holes at the ends of the rollers
and the metal pins inserted, or nuts adjusted, as the case may be, in order to
stretch the material to the right tension.
The raw edges at the sides must now be
turned in or bound with tape, and a string
securely attached at intervals along the
edge; this is for lacing the string through
that now braces the material to the sides
of the frame (see fig. 1). The screw-sided
frame has an advantage over the side pieces
shown in fig. 9, in that in the former an
extra turn can, at this point, be given to the
nuts to still further stretch the material;
on the other hand, some workers prefer
the flat side pieces, thinking that they
make the frame more rigid.

If the material, when fixed to the two
webbings, is too long for the frame, it
must be wound round one of the rollers
until of the correct size. This must be
done carefully, for a delicate fabric might
get damaged in the process; the roller
can be padded with soft paper, and an
interlining of tissue paper can be inserted
and wound up with the material. It may
not always be desirable to do this wind-

ing round the rollers; in that case fine
glazed holland can be stretched in the
frame, and the part to be first embroidered
fixed to it. When the first part of the
work is completed, the holland is cut out
of the frame and fresh pieces substituted
as the work goes on. If it is not wished
that the stitches should be taken through
both surfaces, as would here be the case,
it would be possible to cut the linen partly
away underneath, and use it only as a kind
of inner frame for stretching the material
on, in a way somewhat like that already
described (see fig. 9).

A backing to the material, however,
is often a necessity—perhaps heavy work
may be put on it or the stuff itself is
fragile; in such cases there must be a
backing of some kind. This usually
consists of fine holland or linen, which
is first stretched in the frame and then
has the surface material securely stitched
to it with overcast stitches, care being taken
that both materials are equally strained.

To frame velvet, sew it to the webbing by the selvedges or that way of
the material, since the pile with that
arrangement is more manageable when the
embroidery is in progress.

PART II
TAPESTRY WEAVING

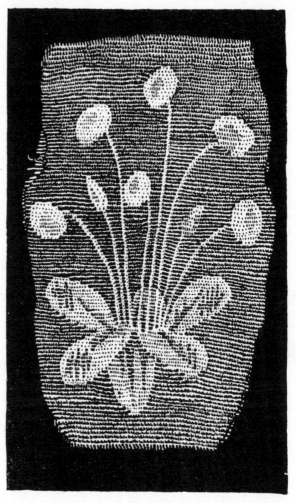

FIG. 168.

PART II

TAPESTRY WEAVING

CHAPTER XV

INTRODUCTION

WEAVING, a most ancient art, naturally precedes embroidery, for this necessitates an already existing ground stuff, which is generally some kind of woven material. All varieties of weaving are done by one little-varied method, that of the weft passing to and fro in and out of the warp, and thus binding the whole into a fabric or web.

The kind of weaving which demands from the worker the greatest artistic skill is that which produced the great masterpieces of Flanders, once known as Arras, from the town of that name, and now commonly called Gobelins tapestry, so

307

named from the *Manufacture des Gobelins* in Paris, at which establishment, founded over three hundred years ago, it is still produced.

It is this kind of weaving that is now to be discussed, but without the least suggestion that the pupil should work upon a scale so large as is usually followed, though there is no reason against doing so if it is practicable. Tapestry weaving is so constantly associated with objects of large size, such as wall hangings, that it is scarcely realised as an art in this smaller way and as an alternative to embroidery. Yet it can be work of a most interesting kind even when produced in pieces only six inches square, as is well shown by existing specimens of the work of the weavers in Egypt who flourished in the early centuries of the Christian era. Examples of this work can be seen in many museums; they consist frequently of decorative panels of tapestry work inlaid in linen tunics and stuffs that have been used as grave clothes. These early Coptic examples are, like all tapestry, built up by interweaving various threads upon warp-strings stretched in close parallel lines. By varying the colour of the threads that are

thus manipulated upon the warp, patterns
of any degree of complexity can be built
up directly by hand, and without the
assistance of any further mechanical contrivance. The peculiarity of this ancient
weaving is that the patterns are frequently
woven upon the warp-threads of some
fabric, from which the weft either has
been removed, or, what is perhaps more
probable, been purposely left out when
the material was made, to leave space
for this decorative pattern weaving to
be added to it.

The Latin name for the workman who
in this way wove in the ornamental patterns was *Plumarius*, which is a name
known to be applied to an embroiderer
also. This weaving of small subjects
is certainly very little removed from embroidery; it may fairly be called needlework, for it is as often carried out with
needles as with bobbins, the former being
frequently better suited to the size of the
work.

In execution weaving is not more
difficult than embroidered work; it can
be done in an ordinary room and upon
a simple loom that is not more cumber-
some than an embroidery frame; in fact

309

an embroidery frame can sometimes be used in the place of a loom.

Weaving takes about as long in doing as finely stitched solid needlework, for in weaving the entire fabric is made, both pattern and ground. The speed with which the work can be done of course varies considerably, being mainly dependent upon the design that is being carried out. Also the quality of the materials used affects the rate of working ; for instance, the thickness of the warp-strings and the placing of them nearer together or further apart. Moreover the weft may be composed of one strand or of several strands together.

In weaving, unless the materials used are very fine, it is impossible to get minute detail in drawing; fortunately it is seldom necessary to attempt much of this. The simpler and more direct work is as good as, and sometimes better than, that with finely gradated colour, shading, and form. On the other hand, work, small in scale, even though simply treated, does not look well when carried out with very coarse materials, for they seem out of proportion to the size of it.

The main difficulty in the technique of

310

the work lies in the attainment of good
draughtsmanship, which of course includes
light and shade as well as outline. It is
naturally more difficult to draw by means
of bobbin and thread, in horizontal lines,
than to work unrestrictedly with a pencil,
or even with an embroidery needle.

There is a great deal in the preparation
of the design; as in all other crafts this
must be suited to the method of work;
otherwise the difficulties of execution will
be greatly increased and the result will be
less satisfactory. This is even more important in weaving than in embroidery,
for in the latter the stitch and method
may possibly be chosen to suit the design,
but in weaving no variation of stitch is
possible; all must be carried out in the
same way.

Tapestry weaving, whether for wall
hangings or for small objects, has the
same technical difficulties, and certain
restrictions govern all work of the kind.
One point to be observed is, the main
lines of the design should go as little as
possible in the same direction as the warp
threads. This is because with each change
of colour in the weft that occurs in the
direction of the warp, there comes an

311

inevitable separation in the woven material, which, oft repeated, would materially impair the strength of the fabric. The less frequently this occurs, of course, the better, since it entails additional labour, either a joining - together stitch at the time of working or an after-sewing up from the back. Long lines made by change of colour going straight or at a slight angle across the warp-threads, are perfectly simple to manage, and the hatching lines of shading, as well as the outline, should be taken as much as possible in this direction.

It will be noticed that most tapestries have the ribbed lines of warp going horizontally across; in the loom these lines are perpendicular, so this means that the design has been placed and carried out sideways upon it. This is for the reason just under discussion, for the long lines of a design are most frequently perpendicular, take, for instance, lines of figures, draperies, or architecture, and so by placing the design sideways in the loom, most of the important lines will come in the direction most easy for the working of them.

With small pieces it frequently does

not matter which way it is carried out,
but it is useful to know when making
the design that there is the alternative of
placing it either way upon the warp-
threads. If this matter were not considered and arranged, there might
come a good deal of twisting
round one or two warp-threads
which would be most unsatisfactory in working and in appearance.
A band of plain colour framing
a square piece of work will be
found to be completely detached
from the centre part upon each
side of the square, although working in very straightforwardly at
the top and base; if, instead of
being a straight band, the inner
edge was vandyked, the work
would be well knitted together
upon all sides (see fig. 169). In
such ways as this the technical
pitfalls can be somewhat avoided
by a designer who understands
the method of the work.

FIG. 169.

To lay down definite rules for designing is practically impossible; right and
wrong depend upon so many circumstances.
The study of fine tapestries of the best

313

periods is one of the most satisfactory
ways of learning what one may or may
not attempt; the beautifully flowered
grounds in many of these show what
excellent motives flowers make, and how
they should be treated. It is not usually
a good plan to introduce in any part
of the work much plain ground, for it
is inclined to look poor; this is very
likely the reason why the grass in tapestry-
land is often covered with such profusion
of flowers. Tapestry calls for beautiful
colour, richness, and plenty of interesting
detail; it is essentially decorative work,
and must be treated as such. The
arrangement of colours and tones need
to be sharply defined; if by chance a
dark leaf comes against another dark
one, a line of light colour is sometimes
deliberately run between, perhaps shading
or outlining one of the forms; a flower
may even change its colour as it passes
over different backgrounds; what is more
remarkable is that this change, unless
sought for, is imperceptible.

The work may be applied to all kinds
of uses, such as coverings for furniture,
mats, curtains, bell - pulls, book-covers,
bags, boxes, and so forth. Anything

that hangs upon a wall is particularly
suitable for working in tapestry, for at a
little distance this kind of work shows up
more effectively than embroidered work
does. A great many articles, such as
alms-bags, frontals of all kinds, stoles and
book-markers, for use in churches could
most excellently be carried out in tapestry.

CHAPTER XVI

NECESSARY APPLIANCES AND MATERIALS

The Loom—Mirror—Bobbins and Needles—The
Comb—Embroidery Frame treated as a Loom—
Warp—Wools—Silk—Gold and Silver Thread.

TOOLS AND APPLIANCES

THE chief requisite for weaving is the
loom; this can be made by a carpenter
from a working drawing. In the Victoria
and Albert Museum there is a model of a
small tapestry loom, presented by William
Morris, which a novice will do well to
examine. It is quite possible to carry
out a small piece of weaving upon an
embroidery frame, but to work in a loom
which has all the proper appliances is

always quicker, better, and absolutely necessary with work of any size.

There are two main varieties of tapestry loom, one in which the warp-threads are horizontal, and another in which they are vertical. The latter kind is considered to give the best results, mainly owing to the possibility of the worker's seeing the right side of the work whilst it is in progress. This is a great advantage, for tapestry is woven with the reverse side towards the worker, and progresses by such gradual steps that the weaver is prone to lose sight of the whole whilst paying attention to the part in progress, and it will be easily understood that to be able to go round and view the entire piece is of immense help. A detail may perhaps be corrected during the progress of the work, but afterwards this would be an awkward matter. It is one of the difficulties of weaving to have to finish completely each step as it comes up. Working from the wrong side is not so hard as it might seem, for both sides are practically alike; the side towards the worker, however, shows ends of thread and thread passing from one place to another, which make it somewhat unpresentable.

316

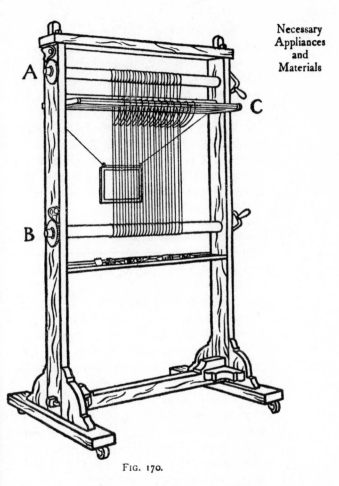

A

B

C

FIG. 170.

317

Fig. 170 shows a drawing of a small loom with some warp stretched upon it in readiness for commencing work. It stands upon the ground, and is about 4 feet high by 2½ feet wide. It is made of beechwood; a hard wood like this is best, for there must be no possibility of the rollers bending with the strain of the warp. The loom consists of two uprights standing upon heavy feet; these uprights are joined together at the top

FIG. 171.

and base by strengthening cross bars. Two wooden rollers are fixed into the uprights (see A and B in fig 170) and in the surface of each of these a narrow groove is hollowed out lengthwise (see fig. 171); this is for the purpose of holding a long metal pin, by means of which the warp-threads are kept in place. The rollers are fitted at one extremity with a handle for turning them round, and at the other with a ratchet and toothed wheel to prevent unwinding. The pur-

318

pose of the upper roller is to hold the supply of warp-thread and unwind it as required; the lower one is for winding up the web as the work progresses, so that upon a loom of this size a piece of work of considerable length can easily be carried out.

The warp soon after it passes from the top roller is divided into two leaves by a cylindrical wooden bar about one inch

FIG. 172.

in diameter, called the cross stave (see fig. 172). The cross stave may be oval or round in section; if it is oval the warp-threads may be moved more widely apart when required by turning the stave round, but this is not often necessary. The upper part of the cross stave can be seen in position in the loom diagram, which shows also how the stave divides the threads, which pass alternately one in front and one behind the bar. After this the threads are passed through a comb-like instru-

319

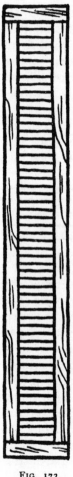

FIG. 173.

ment, having about fourteen divisions to the inch (see fig. 173). This extends from side to side of the loom, and lies in a groove made in the bar that fixes the coat-stave (C in fig. 170) in position at either extremity. It can be taken out and exchanged for another with a different divisioning, if necessary; without doing this, however, it is quite possible to put at intervals two threads through one division, or to pass over one occasionally if need be. The threads are next fixed in the lower roller.

The coat-stave can be seen projecting from near the top of the loom. A number of looped threads called coats are fixed to it, and each one of these encircles a thread of the warp. They are attached only to those threads that were passed behind the cross stave and form the back

leaf of the warp, and they are for the purpose of pulling these forward when required.

Underneath the lower roller is fixed a
wooden tray, which is useful for holding
bobbins, comb, or scissors.

On the loom is hung a small mirror
facing the right side of the work (see fig.
170). This enables the weaver to glance
now and then through the warp-strings
at any detail that is in progress.

Smaller looms can be made, suitable

FIG. 174.

for placing upon a table; these, standing about two feet in height, must in
some way be firmly fixed to the table,
in order to be properly rigid for work.

The thread composing the woof is
wound upon a wooden bobbin or shuttle,
such as that shown in fig. 174. The
chief point about this is, that it may not
have sharp angles that might catch in
the warp whilst passing to and fro. The
pointed end is sometimes made use of
to poke between the warp-threads and

321

press down the weft. A fresh bobbin is employed for each colour, and the wool is wound upon it two or three strands together, just as may happen to be

FIG. 175.

required for the work. Large blunt-pointed needles about three inches long (fig. 175) are often used in place of bobbins, for with small pieces of work

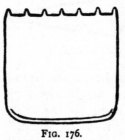

sometimes so little of a colour is required as to make it unnecessary to wind a quantity on a bobbin, which is, after all, only a needle with an extra long thread.

A comb is necessary for pressing down

FIG. 176.

the weft whilst the work is in progress. Combs vary in size and shape; fig. 176 shows one suitable for this type of work; it is 1½ inches square, slightly wedge-shaped, and about one-eighth of an inch thick. Boxwood is the most suitable wood to make them from, since it is

322

particularly hard and fine in the grain. They are sometimes made of metal,

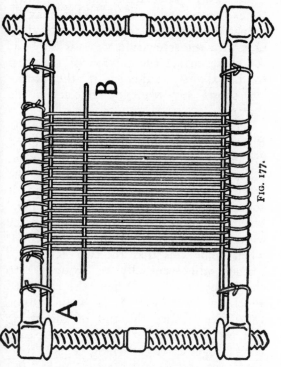

B

A

FIG. 177.

ivory, or bone; for large work, metal combs of a heavier type are used.

An embroidery frame, which has been

already mentioned as a possible substitute for the loom, is oftentimes an article more easily procured. Fig. 177 illustrates how a frame of this kind may be prepared with warp-threads for weaving. One with the screw side pieces is the best, for these enable the tension of the warp to be slightly adjusted if the working shows any tendency to slacken the thread.

To prepare the frame for weaving— Place the parts together at the required distance from each other; secure the end of some warp-thread to some part of the frame, and then commence to wind it round and round over the two rollers, placing the threads at approximately the right distance apart, taking into account when doing this that the two leaves thus formed will eventually be brought into the same plane. When the required width of warp-thread is wound upon the rollers, secure the end of the string and proceed to bring the front and back leaves together by darning a knitting-needle or some similar article in and out of the threads at the centre. Then slide it up close to the top roller and secure it by tying it with string at each end (see diagram). The same process is gone through with a second pin, which is tied to the lower roller.

The warp-threads can now be adjusted to their proper distance apart, as they will probably be a little irregularly spaced. The next process is to weave two or three courses of warp-thread close to the knitting-pins at either end; this brings the warp still nearer to being in the one plane, and enables the threads to be arranged in perfect order by the aid of the point of the bobbin or a needle, and they will remain as now placed.

The frame is now ready for work. A piece of plain web, about half an inch in width, is usually woven before the actual design is begun; this serves as a selvedge for turning in when the completed work is mounted, and also gets the warp into condition much better for working upon.

A thick knitting-needle can be passed between the alternate threads of the warp and placed towards the top of the frame, as shown in the diagram. This takes the place of the cross-stave in the loom, and, by thus dividing the warp into two leaves, is of assistance when the shuttle goes in one direction. Coats cannot easily be applied to an embroidery frame.

It is quite possible upon a frame of this kind to weave a long narrow band of any kind. The warp must be wound on and arranged in position at the necessary length by separating the rollers and temporarily fixing them apart at the distance required for the band. The surplus warp is then wound up on the upper roller until the side pieces will fit into the ends. As it gets worked upon, the completed part is wound upon the lower roller. A piece both long and wide would be impracticable, especially if any winding on and off the rollers were necessary.

MATERIALS

There are very few materials required for tapestry weaving ; they consist of, string for warp, wools, silks, and maybe gold and silver thread for the weft.

The warp is usually composed of a smooth, strong, evenly twisted thread, specially made for the purpose. It can be procured of various thicknesses. It happens sometimes that in parts the warp shows, as a fringe or in some other

326

way; in this case it could be made of a strong silk thread, such as purse silk, though for edges of mats, the ordinary string warp fringed out is quite suitable. Occasionally weaving is carried out in such a way as to expose the warp in various parts of the work, the pattern being woven, but the ground left altogether unworked. In a case of this kind the colour and composition of the warp is naturally important, and must be considered. In a show-case in the British Museum there can be seen a small book with an interesting woven binding carried out after this manner. The warp is composed of gold passing, and the effect of this with a pattern carried out in brightly coloured silks is very pretty indeed, the gold adding a rich glow to the whole.

Wool and silk are the chief materials used for the woof. It is well to choose those of fine texture, for several strands can then be wound together upon one bobbin, which, with coarse materials, would be too clumsy a method. When working in this way there is more opportunity of varying colour and texture, for three shades may be wound upon the bobbin together to get a required colour,

327

and this has often a prettier effect than the use of an unblended colour; also, silk and wool are very satisfactory wound and worked in together, each texture showing the other to advantage.

Fine gold or silver threads are frequently used in tapestry weaving. They can be woven in alone, which gives a metallic look, or they may be mixed with strands of silk. Both ways are very good, and the use of the metal thread adds great richness to the work. These threads make fine backgrounds, and they can be used in many ways upon the design; it is a common practice to carry out the lighting of draperies and of other parts in real gold, just as they are treated in illuminated manuscripts.

CHAPTER XVII

PREPARATIONS FOR WORK

Warping the Loom—Dressing the Coat-Stave—
Tracing the Pattern upon the Threads.

UPON commencing the warping of the loom the first matter to be decided is the length of the threads. Some extra length must be measured off besides that

328

actually used for weaving, to allow for what is taken up in fixing the threads and winding them round the rollers, and as it is not convenient to work more than about half-way up the loom, this also has to be allowed for in the length. The threads must all be cut to one size, and since they have to be doubled in halves when placed on the loom, this should be twice the required length.

Another question for early decision is the number of warp-threads that may be allowed per inch. This varies with the coarseness of the strings and the thickness of the weft that will have to pass to and fro between them; what governs both of these points is the design, whether there is much detail or not, for if the drawing is complicated the warp-strings must be fine in order to be able to carry it out; this point will be better understood after some experience of working. Fourteen to sixteen threads to the inch is a very usual number.

The fixing of the threads in the upper roller is a very simple matter. It is done by doubling each in halves and placing the loop thus formed over the metal pin, which for this purpose may be temporarily suspended by string to the frame of the top

of the loom just above the roller. It can
be dropped into its place in the groove
when all the threads are looped upon it,
and made secure there for the moment by
tying some string round the extremities
of the roller.

Each thread is now taken separately
through the comb-like instrument. The
cross-stave is laid upon this, so it is well
to put it in place now, and carry the
threads alternately in front and behind it,
whilst passing them through the comb.
The threading of the strings through the
comb decides the number there will be to
the inch, so they must be put through at
the required distance apart.

The upper roller is next given a complete turn, which will make the metal
pin and the threads that are round it
secure in the groove. The winding up
must be continued until only about three
inches of the warp-string hang below the
lower roller. Some kind of tension must
be applied to the threads whilst this
winding is going on, or it will be done
irregularly; a hand, or several hands, holding it, answers the purpose well enough.

The next process is to fix the threads
securely in the lower roller. The diffi-

330

culty here lies in getting the placing and tension of the threads between the two rollers exactly regular and even. If some

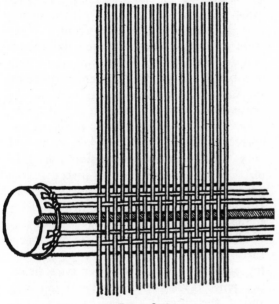

FIG. 178.

were slack and others tight it would be very awkward to correct afterwards, and impossible to weave upon properly if incorrect.

Fig. 178 shows a practical method by

which the warp may be fixed in the lower roller, but any contrivance will do that gains the required result. To carry out the fixing as in the diagram, the roller must be turned so that the groove comes just at the centre in the front. Four lines of warp-thread are then fixed from end to end of the roller, two above and two below the groove. Each warp-string in turn is now threaded in and out of these cross lines, as shown in the diagram. This places them in regular order, at the correct distance apart, and keeps them at very nearly the same tension throughout. The metal pin is now placed in the groove and pushes the threads before it. It must be temporarily made firm there by string tied round the roller at intervals.

The next process is to tie the warp-threads in knots, either two or four together, just where they emerge below the pin. This prevents any giving way, and if the threads are pulled just equally tight immediately before the knotting, the tension of the entire warp will be the same. The lower roller is next turned round until the metal pin is made quite firm in its place by the warp-threads passing across the face of the groove. The

332

warp will now be fixed in the loom as shown in the drawing in fig. 170.

The placing of the coats upon the coat-stave is the next part of the preparatory work. Commence by fixing a line of warp-thread along the exterior side of the coat-stave, making it secure to the bar at both ends. The coats, encircling the stave and a thread of warp, are fixed to this string by a kind of button-hole stitch (see fig. 179). It is important that each loop should be of exactly the same size; this can be ensured by temporarily fixing a rod across the loom at the point where the loops will encircle the warp-thread, and then taking the loop round this bar as well as round the thread.

To commence making the coats, take a long needleful of warp-thread and secure the end of it to the string at the right-hand end, and then make about three small looped stitches upon it (see needle in progress in the diagram); next, instead of making another of the same stitches, take the thread down below the stave, let it encircle the first thread of the back leaf and then be brought up over the coat-stave and string and be

333

looped under the thread to complete the

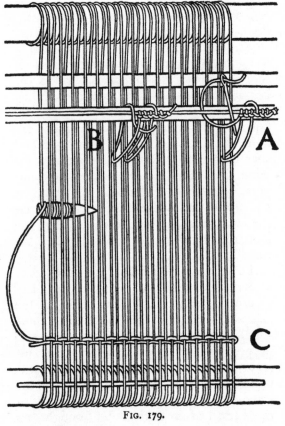

FIG. 179.

stitch (see B).   Usually a long and a

334

short stitch are taken alternately, but the number of short ones may be varied. This process is continued until all the threads of the back leaf are encircled each by a loop.

A new length of thread must be knotted on to the last one as it gets used up. The weavers' knot, which is shown on p. 291, might be used for the purpose. It would be made use of also if by chance the warp-thread were broken, for it is a knot specially good for the purpose.

When the coats are completed there are still one or two preparations to be made before actually commencing to weave. Either a metal rod or a long narrow piece of wood must now be threaded in and out of the warp-strings and placed in position at the base. This rod can be seen properly placed in position in fig. 179 in front of the lower cylinder. This is put there to keep the lines of the woof horizontal when they are being beaten down by the comb.

Next wind on a bobbin some warp-thread similar to that already on the loom, or, if that happens to be very coarse, let this be a little finer. Now weave two courses with this warp-thread and beat it down with the comb, leaving the woof during the process rather loose   The technique of weaving with all its

335

difficulties is discussed in Chapter XVIII.
When two of the warp-thread courses are
complete, insert either the pointed end of
the bobbin or a blunt needle between the
warp-threads below the woven portion, and
if necessary move the warp-strings a little
to or fro until they are equally separated
each from the other all along the line. Next
weave about four more courses of the woof;
these will serve to keep the arranged warp-
threads still more firmly in place. Then
with a red pencil rule a horizontal line
straight across the warp-strings about one-
third of an inch above the woven portion.
Wind on another bobbin some wool and
weave it to and fro until the space between
the woven portion and the red line is filled
in. Between each course the comb must
beat the woof-threads firmly down. It is
often necessary to weave over some portions
of the surface more than over others as the
threads pack down tighter in some parts.
The loom should be now in perfect order
for commencing work. The preparatory
weaving that has been done is often useful
afterwards as a selvedge.

It is necessary to have a coloured
drawing of the design for frequent reference whilst the work is in progress; also

a tracing of the outline must be marked
upon the warp-threads for the worker's
further guidance. The tracing upon the
threads must be a reflection of the pattern
owing to the fact that the work is done
from the back. It does not affect the
matter if the design is a symmetrical one,
but to find the lions of England facing
the wrong way in some completed piece of
heraldic work would be most annoying. In
order to get a tracing of the design upon
the threads, a sheet of paper, with a distinct outline of the pattern upon it, must
be attached, possibly by pinning, to the
further side of the warp-threads, exactly
where the weaving is to take place. The
outline will be clearly perceivable through
the threads, and the next process is to take
pen and Indian ink and make a dot upon
each warp-thread in sequence round the
outline of the pattern. When this is completed, the tracing-paper can be removed,
and the dots upon the warp must be taken all
round each thread instead of marking one side
only. The marking round is done by holding
a warp-thread between the finger and thumb,
placing the side of the nib against one of the
dots, and then twisting the thread to and fro
against it. All the marks upon the first

337

thread are treated in succession in this way,
then the next thread is taken up and

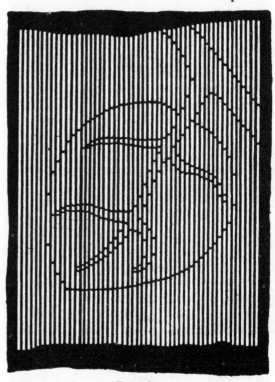

Fig. 180.

treated in similar fashion, and so on until
all are done. Fig. 180 shows a leaf marked

upon the warp-threads in readiness for working. This marking should be clear, sharp, and decided, all the lines being taken horizontally round, as in fig. 180; if the pattern seems to run up a thread, a mark just half-way up is sufficient guide. In a piece of work of any size the tracing must be done, a part at a time, for the threads moving slightly when the warp is unwound and the web wound up may displace the marks and make the guiding lines incorrect.

CHAPTER XVIII

THE TECHNIQUE OF WEAVING

Weaving—Commencing and Fastening Off—The Interlocking Stitch—Fine Drawing—Shading—Added After-stitches.

THE way in which the woof threading in and out of the warp makes the web is shown at C, fig. 179. Here the woof has been taken once to and fro; a movement called a weft or a course, one way only, goes by the name of a half pass or a shoot. By the use of the cross stave for one direction, and of the coats for the other, the tediousness of the process of

339

darning in and out and so picking up the right threads is avoided. It is not always practical to make use of these appliances; for instance, in working over only two or three threads it may not be worth while, but when they can be made use of the work is done twice as rapidly by their help.

The bobbin enters the loom rather high up, for there the division of threads is greatest. One hand starts the bobbin upon its journey, the other hand, entering between the divided warp-threads, takes it on and out as required. Sometimes the bobbin has to go the entire way between the leaves, and at others it may be only over two or three threads, this depending upon the pattern. To enable the bobbin to make the return passage, the warp must be redivided, the threads that are at the back must be brought to the front; this is managed by the help of the coats—a bunch of them is taken in the hand in order to pull forward the threads to which they are attached. This can be done by sections all along the line, or just in one part of it if it be so required.

The weft is almost always taken in horizontal lines to and fro. The exceptions to this rule occur when it is very

340

evident that to run up and down a narrow slanting line from end to end is far simpler than to work up in a horizontal zigzag fashion along it.

About an inch of thread is left at the end and at the commencement of each length of weft; these are secured by the tight packing down of the threads above them, so there is as a rule no need for any knot or fastening off, which would be necessary only in the case of commencing or ending off round a single thread, but it is important for the future durability of the work to see that the ends are secured. Sometimes a commencement or a finish is made just where a natural division of the fabric occurs; in this case, the end of thread would not be secure, for it might work loose or appear upon the right side. This can usually be avoided by commencing a little further along the line. The few times that fastening off or on is necessary, the thread can be run into the part already woven with a smaller needle, or else be knotted on to a loose end of wool.

The bobbins not actually in use hang down fixed as in lace work by a half-hitch. Fig. 181 shows this in process of making; the loop is passed from the

341

finger on to the bobbin; it will unwind
as wanted and yet hold firm whilst hanging down. The thread is always carried,
if practicable, from one place to where
it is next required, in order to avoid unnecessary breaking off. Tapestry is sometimes woven with both sides alike, which

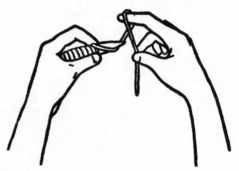

FIG. 181.

means only that all the ends must be cut
close off. It is said that work so treated
is quite durable.

Special care must be taken that the weft is
turned neatly round at the margins, because
if it is at all loose there the work has a
ragged, untidy appearance. This applies
also to any turnings that may occur in other
parts due to the carrying out of the pattern;

342

ıf in these places the thread is too loose
upon the warp, the fabric will be uneven
and pushed out of place; if on the other
hand the thread there is too tight, the
slits will gape, and if these are afterwards
closed by stitching, the entire material
will be drawn in. A new thread is never
commenced actually at the margin, for it
would then be seen upon the right side;
it is quite easy to avoid this happening
by commencing an inch further in. This
may entail beginning in a direction which
is apparently wrong for picking up the
proper threads, that is, those not picked
up in the row below; but this must happen
at times, and the work packs down and
quite prevents the warp showing, as it
might be inclined to do in such a case. It
is sometimes at the margin a good plan to
pick up two warp-threads together, for
this emphasises the edge rather pleasantly;
this might be advisable in carrying out a
long ribbon-like border of any kind.

After each shoot, the point of the
bobbin, the comb, or maybe the fingers,
should press down the woof to make it
lie close upon the row before, and so
entirely cover up the warp. Fig. 182
shows the comb in action, and also the

343

bobbins hanging.   The weft must be left
a little slack along the line for this purpose, and some experience is required in
order to leave just the right slackness.
The turn at the edge is arranged first,
and then the thread eased evenly along

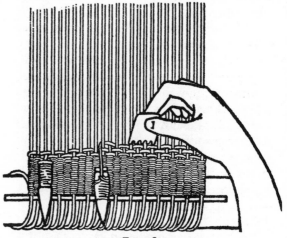

FIG. 182.

its length in readiness for being pressed
down; it must have the appearance not of
running straight across the warp-strings,
but of lying loosely round them.   For
packing down a long line, much more play
of weft is required than for a short one.

344

The usual fault with beginners is to draw the web too tight here and there. This is a fault to be specially avoided, for it causes the fabric to be drawn in, and to vary in width, spoiling its appearance and making the threads difficult to work upon; also the packing down of the weft could not be properly done, which would cause the warp-threads to be exposed in parts.

The thoroughness of this packing down of the weft is for several reasons very important. The durability of the work is much affected by it, both for the securing of the ends of wool already mentioned, and for the making of a strong, well-knit piece of fabric. Another reason is, that the drawing of the various forms in the design may be made incorrect, in this way: suppose an apple were woven in, apparently correctly, but the wefts were not pressed down thoroughly, the weaving and packing down of the wefts above it would be sure to press the part underneath closer together, and the effect of this would be to make the round apple assume a flattened oval shape, and cause similar changes throughout the work.

It has already been mentioned that wher-

345

ever a change of colour occurs vertically, that is, in the direction of the warp-threads, there results of necessity a division or slit in the web; the slit, which may be of any length, if noticeable, must be closed. This can be done whilst the weaving is in progress by a method of interlocking the two wefts as they meet, or else by stitching up at the back when the work is finished. The latter way is called fine drawing, and must be very carefully done, especially with large tapestries.

Both methods are used; the first takes longer, but is the most durable. Old and worn tapestries will usually be seen to have given way where this stitching up at the back has taken place. In small pieces of work, however, there is not much likelihood of strain, so the oversewing at the back answers fairly well. The two ways can be used in conjunction. Supposing a border, owing to its being of a different colour, had to be joined the entire length of the work, the interlocking stitches might be made at intervals of about half an inch, and when the work was finished the oversewing at the back might be taken the entire length.

Fig. 183 is a diagram illustrating the
346

way in which the wefts may be interlocked whilst the weaving goes on. Examination of the drawing will probably be sufficient explanation; however, interlocking is effected thus: Commencing at the base, run a weft of the darker wool to and fro, leaving it slack at the turning point. A half pass of the lighter-coloured woof is

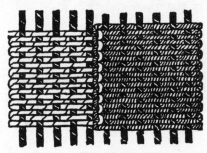

Fig. 183.

then run through, it is threaded in an upward direction through the slack loop of the darker wool, waits there whilst another weft of the darker colour is worked, and then is threaded down through the second loop that has been formed, and returns to the starting-point. It then comes back again and is threaded upwards through this same loop, and waits, as before, for another to be formed, and

returns back through it—and so on. If
this is done properly, no change is visible
on the right side. The joined weft will last
as long as any other part of the weaving.

The process of stitching up at the back
is simply an oversewing with silk or other
strong thread. The stitches must be
rather close, drawing the edges just sufficiently together, and they must not show

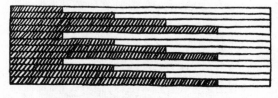

Fig. 184.

through to the right side. The stitching
together should be done while the work is
on the loom, since the web would then be
in less danger of pulling out of shape.

Shading in tapestry weaving is carried
out by a hatching process which is most
simply explained by a diagram (fig. 184).
The difficulty is not in the working, but
in getting the form of the shadow or
light correctly expressed. There is no
need for fine gradation of colour and tone,

348

for the shading looks best when carried out simply and boldly, but the drawing of it should be decided and good. The above figure gives but one intermediary tone in shading from one colour to another, which is the ancient method of working ; at the present day the weavers in the *Manufacture des Gobelins* employ several other intermediary tones, thus allowing of finer gradation ; possibly however these fine gradations are not of such great importance, and so need not have an unnecessary amount of attention and time devoted to their accomplishment.

The student will do well to examine fine examples and make careful drawings from them, since this will teach the right way of going to work better than anything else can. Fig. 185 is simply a shaded leaf taken at random from a piece of weaving ; the same leaf was shown in outline in fig. 180, so the two show the commencement and completion of the same piece. It will be noticed upon studying tapestry that usually all the light parts of a work are hatched with the same colour, often a buff shade, those of rich tapestries with gold thread. This sameness of colour throughout gives unity to the work.

349

Sometimes after the weaving is completed a few finishing touches can be satisfactorily put in by means of single stitches taken through the fabric with a sharp-

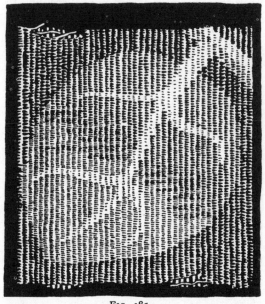

Fig. 185.

pointed embroidery needle. The dots representing the seeds upon a strawberry could be stitched in afterwards in this way, for to insert them while the work is going on would be very tedious. This

350

kind of thing must not be overdone, however, for the stitches are apt, unless very deftly treated, to have a laid-on look, and care must be taken not to mar the evenly ribbed effect, which is one of the characteristics of tapestry.

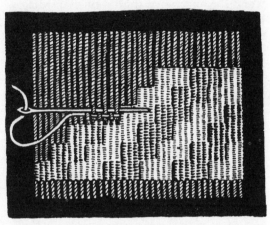

FIG. 186.

This weaving is a most fascinating kind of work, as will be found upon a trial. The simplest patterns look very interesting when woven, and, on the other hand, the work can be carried to any degree of complexity that the worker desires. For a first trial a piece might

351

be done with no attempt at shading; even one such as that illustrated at fig. 186 would be suitable. This example happens to be a form particularly easy for carrying out in weaving. The worker should begin at the lower right-hand corner and work the successive flights of steps diagonally, as shown by the unfinished portion of the diagram.

In the way of actual technique there is in the art of tapestry weaving not nearly as must to be learnt as there is in embroidery, for there are no varieties of methods and of stitch to be acquired; still for a person to become a skilled weaver, capable of carrying out large wall hangings, is a thing very difficult of attainment—indeed it is said that it takes as long as fifteen years of constant application to acquire the necessary knowledge and skill. To carry out designs of less magnitude and intricacy is a very different matter; success in this smaller way is far more easily attained, and is well within the reach of unprofessional people.

NOTES ON THE
COLLOTYPE PLATES

NOTES ON THE
COLLOTYPE PLATES

PLATE I.—*A Detail from a XIVth Century English Cope.*—The figure of Christ which is shown in this plate is taken from a central group, representing the coronation of the Virgin, in a famous cope in the possession of Colonel J. E. Butler-Bowdon. The ground is of rich red silk velvet; the face, hands, and linings of the draperies are worked in silk in split stitch; the drapery, crown, and surrounding architectural decoration are in gold thread couched by the early method. The twisted column with oak leaves and the five lobed arch are both characteristic of English work of this period. Note the use of pearls in the lion's head and in the acorns, also the charmingly drawn bird. An interesting technical point displayed in this example is that the work is done directly on to the velvet ground, instead of being first worked upon linen and afterwards as a completed piece of embroidery applied to the velvet. The method in use here, if at all possible, is always the most satisfactory.

Size of detail, about eleven inches by six.

PLATE II.—*Two Heads from a XIVth Century English Cope preserved at Steeple Aston, Oxfordshire.* — The cope is not now in its original state, for it has been divided into two parts and used for the decoration of the altar. The background is composed of a thin greyish white silk backed with a stronger material. The white may have been originally some other colour; it is, however, in its present state, very beautiful and harmonious. The drawing of the features in this cope is remarkably refined and true to nature (the reproduction does not do full justice to the original). The ancient method, of working the faces in split stitch commencing with the middle of the cheek and continuing spirally round, then afterwards pressing the centre down by some mechanical means, is plainly to be observed here.

356

The effective drawing of the tresses of hair in alternate lines of two colours is well seen in the left-hand example. The gold thread which is freely made use of all over the cope, upon the draperies, nimbi, and surrounding foliage, is marvellously bright and sparkling, although nearly six hundred years old. The manufacture of untarnishable gold for embroidery purposes seems beyond present day enterprise.

Width of nimbus, two and a half inches.

PLATE III.—*A small portion of a Quilted Coverlet, probably of Sicilian work. Date about* 1400.—In this interesting example of quilting, which is exhibited in the Victoria and Albert Museum, the ground is composed of a buff-coloured linen. The raised effect is obtained by an interpadding of wool. The background is run over irregularly with white thread, in order to keep it more or less flat, and the design, which is in fairly high relief, is outlined with brown thread. The entire coverlet is embroidered with scenes from the life of Tristan. Tristan frequently engaged in battle against King Languis, the oppressor of his country.

357

This detail represents "How King Languis
(of Ireland) sent to Cornwall for the
tribute."

Size of detail, two feet by three.

PLATE IV.—*A portion of an Altar Cloth
Band, embroidered in coloured silk threads
upon a white linen ground.*—This is a piece
of German XVth century work exhibited
in the Victoria and Albert Museum. It
is embroidered almost entirely in one stitch,
which might be described as a variety of
herring-bone. The design is made up of
two motives which repeat alternately along
the band—a square shaped tree and a circle,
the latter decorated with floral sprays and,
in the centre of it, a group of emblems.
Down the middle of the design runs a
series of names in fine Gothic lettering—
"Ursula" and "Augustinus" being the
two that occur in this plate.

Width of embroidered band, four and a
half inches.

PLATE V.—*A portion of a late XVth century Orphrey, embroidered with the arms of
Henry Stafford, Duke of Buckingham.*—The
358

ground is of red velvet, and is embroidered with gold thread and coloured silks. The two shields here represented bear the arms of the families of de Bohun and Fitzwalter. Each shield has for supporters two swans, and is surrounded by floral sprays. The Stafford knot unites the sprays between the shields. The chasuble upon which this orphrey is placed is made of a lovely brocaded silk decorated with falcons, peahens, and roses.

Width of embroidered orphrey, about eight inches.

PLATE VI.—*A detail of Foliage taken from a late XVIth century Embroidered Picture representing the story of Daphne.*—The picture is worked in coloured wools and silks in cross stitch upon canvas, and is an admirable example of this kind of work, and this particular detail is a good illustration of a very satisfactory treatment of foliage. The whole panel measures about seven feet by two, and is exhibited in the Victoria and Albert Museum.

Height of detail, ten and a half inches.

PLATE VII.—*An Embroidered XVIIth
or XVIIIth century Wool-work Curtain.*—
This curtain, the property of Miss Killick,
is a pretty example of a small crewel-work
hanging. The design is of a type that was
often used upon hangings of that period.
It is embroidered with brightly coloured
wools upon a white linen ground, and is
in a good state of preservation. Much
ingenuity as well as variety of stitching
are shown in the execution of the work.

Size of curtain, about five feet by three.

PLATE VIII.—*A portion of a large XVIIth
century Linen Hanging embroidered with
coloured wools.*—In both design and execution this curtain is remarkably fine. The
entire hanging is about eighteen feet in
width by seven in height. It is embroidered
with a conventional representation of a
forest; in the branches of the trees lodge
all kinds of birds and beasts. The type of
design shown in this plate and in the last
is derived from Eastern work; its introduction into England was due to the increase of trade with oriental nations, which
developed about this time.

Size of detail, about six feet by four.

PLATE IX. — *Cutwork Lettering taken
from a XVIIth century English Sampler.*—
The letters and surrounding decoration
shown in this example of cut or open work
are built up on a square network of warp
and weft threads that were left at regular
intervals throughout the space, when
the unnecessary threads were withdrawn,
and then covered with a kind of darning
stitch. The letters are worked in buttonhole stitch, each fresh line being taken
into the heading of the last one. The
other parts of the work are carried out
in either buttonhole or overcast stitch.
The complete sampler is a long narrow
strip of linen, across which run specimen
bands of various kinds of work. It is
exhibited in the Victoria and Albert
Museum.

Width of cutwork detail, six inches.

PLATE X.—*An Embroidered Sampler.*—
The work is carried out in coloured silks
in minute cross-stitch and occasional rows
of satin stitch, upon a ground of fine
single-thread canvas. It is dated 1798,
and was worked by Alice Knight, the
author's great-grandmother. The birds,

361

trees, and flowers, the charming little
border patterns, and the comical cats
standing on either hillocks or housetops,
are all characteristic of sampler work.
Working the sampler was once the regular
introduction to mending, marking, and
embroidery, and one was done by almost
every XVIIIth century child as a part of
education, indeed the practice of working
samplers was continued some decades into
the XIXth century.

Actual size of original, eighteen inches
by twelve.

PLATE XI.—*An Example of Persian
Embroidery.*—Formerly in the collection
of Lord Leighton, and now in that of the
London County Council's Central School
of Arts and Crafts. The embroidery is
carried out almost entirely in chain stitch
with brilliantly coloured silks, upon a fine
semi - transparent ground. The flowers
that appear dark in the reproduction are
worked in a bright rosy red, others are
yellow and orange, and the leaves are in
pale grey green outlined with a dark
myrtle shade of the same.

Size of panel, about five feet by four.

362

Plate XII.—*A Detail from an Em-broidered Tablecloth.*—The entire surface of this fine white linen cloth is strewn with a profusion of beautiful flowers, worked in floss silk in bright colours. The flowers were all drawn directly from nature by the worker, Mrs. W. R. Lethaby.

Plate XIII.—*An Embroidered Altar Frontal, executed by Miss May Morris, de-signed by Mr. Philip Webb.*—The work is carried out with floss silk in bright colours and gold thread, both background and pattern being embroidered. The five crosses, that are placed at regular intervals between the vine leaves, are couched in gold passing upon a silvery silk ground.

Plate XIV.—*Two Pieces of Ancient Weaving taken from Tombs in Egypt.*—These are exhibited in the Victoria and Albert Museum. The upper example is about five inches square, dated IIIrd to VIIth century, Egypto-Roman work, and is said to have decorated a child's tunic. It is woven in coloured silks upon a green ground; the colours are still wonderfully fresh and bright. Weavers may see various interesting technical as well as other points in this early work. For instance, how the difficulty of the narrow detached vertical lines, necessitated by change of colour in the weft, has been overcome by using surface stitching instead, the easier horizontal lines being woven in the usual way. A good deal of this surface stitching can be seen in the ancient weaving; sometimes an entire pattern is picked out by this method, the ground having been first woven all over in some plain colour.

The lower border pattern is a band of weaving about two inches in width, Saracenic work. It is woven in coloured silks and linen thread upon the actual warp threads of the garment that it decorates. The weft threads were probably omitted for the space of one and a half inches when the fabric was being made in order that some ornamentation might be put in, in this way. Some of the weft threads have perished, leaving the warp exposed to sight; this enables the student to understand better the manner in which it was carried out.

PLATE XV.—*An Example of a Tapestry Field strewn with Flowers.*—This kind of decoration is characteristic of many tapestry grounds, for the style is particularly suited to the method of work, and very happy in result. The detail shown in this plate is taken from a piece of late XVIth century Flemish work ; it carries on, however, a much earlier tradition. The ground is of a dark blue colour, and the flowers varied as in nature.

PLATE XVI.—*A Tapestry Bag, woven in coloured silk and gold thread by the Author.*—The ground is woven with black silk, decorated with gold at the top and base. The centre panel is carried out in brightly coloured silks and gold thread. The various compartments are filled with representations of flowers, birds, and fishes, upon an alternating purple and blue background. The dividing lines are of gold thread.

Size of bag, ten inches by six.

THE COLLOTYPE PLATES

Plates originally printed in collotype are now produced in half-tone.

Plate I.—A detail from a XIVth Century English Cope

Plate II.—Two Heads from a XIVth Century English Cope preserved at Steep
Aston, Oxfordshire.

Plate III.—A small portion of a Quilted Coverlet, probably of Sicilian work.
Date about 1400.

Plate IV.—A portion of an Altar Cloth Band, embroidered in coloured silk threads upon a white linen ground.

Plate V.—A portion of a late XVth Century Orphrey, embroidered with the arms of Henry Stafford, Duke of Buckingham.

Plate VI.—A detail of Foliage taken from a late XVIth Century
Embroidered Picture, representing the story of Daphne.

Plate VII.—An Embroidered XVIIth or XVIIIth Century
Wool-work Curtain.

Plate VIII.—A portion of a large XVIIth Century Linen Hanging, embroidered with coloured wools.

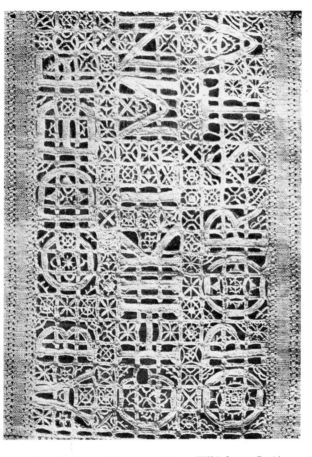

Plate IX.—Cutwork Lettering taken from a XVIIth Century English
Sampler.

Plate X.—An Embroidered Sampler.

Plate XI.—An example of Persian Embroidery.

Plate XII.—A detail from an Embroidered Tablecloth. Designed and executed by Mrs. W. R. Lethaby.

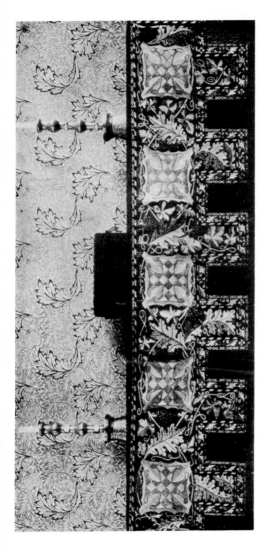

Plate XIII. An Embroidered Altar Frontal, executed by Miss May Morris, designed by Mr. Philip Webb.

Plate XIV.—Two pieces of Ancient Weaving taken from
Tombs in Egypt.

Plate XV.—An example of a Tapestry Field strewn with Flowers.

Plate XVI.—A Tapestry Bag, woven in coloured silk and gold thread by the Author.

INDEX

INDEX

368